2

LIFE BETWEEN DEATH
P. 15 & 16

AND REBIRTH
P. 25

P. 170

Rosemary   110 · 111
190 ·

203 — Asbergers?
226 × 227
245

LIFE BETWEEN DEATH
AND REBIRTH

Sixteen Lectures
by
RUDOLF STEINER

Anthroposophic Press

Translated from shorthand reports un-
revised by the lecturer, from the German edition published with the title,
*Okkulte Untersuchungen über das Leben
zwischen Tod und neuer Geburt* (Vol.
140 in the Bibliographical Survey, 1961).
Translated by R. M. Querido.

Published in the United States of America by Anthroposophic Press,

Library of Congress Catalog No. 68-57429

ISBN: 978-0-910142-62-5

FOREWORD

This is one of many courses of lectures given by Rudolf Steiner (1861–1925) in the early years of this century, in the amplification of his *spiritual science* or *anthroposophy*. Some of these courses were given to members of the Anthroposophical Society who had been familiar with the subject for many years. Others were given to the general public. In both cases —and naturally more particularly and esoterically so in the former—they were a deepening and extension of what was contained in his written works.

It is the written works that contain the essentials of his teaching. Among them are some which have come to be known as the "basic books," and without some knowledge of them it is impossible to appreciate what was spoken of in these lecture courses. Those basic books are: *The Philosophy of Freedom* (also published as *The Philosophy of Spiritual Activity*), *Theosophy, An Outline of Occult Science, Knowledge of the Higher Worlds and Its Attainment,* and *Christianity as Mystical Fact* (also published as *Christianity and Occult Mysteries of Antiquity*).

It is essential to make this clear to readers, and even to impress upon them the need to have some familiarity with the basic books before attempting the courses. The reasons should be obvious. First, it would be unfair to the readers themselves to be led into buying a book which they might find mystifying and confusing, if not wholly incomprehensible, later; and secondly, and perhaps more importantly, it would be unfair to the cause of spiritual science if the unadvised reader should be led to forming a premature judgment about what is admittedly recondite, if not at times arcane, through insufficient knowledge of its basic principles.

Any scientific investigation—and anthroposophy is just that, even though its field is the supersensible—presupposes a discipline which demands a thorough grounding in its fundamentals. This was all Rudolf Steiner ever asked for the results of his investigations, which he gave out in these and other lectures. So finally, it would be unfair to his unchallenged reputation as a scholar and philosopher to offer to the public such a book as this without these few introductory remarks.

Alan Howard

EDITOR'S NOTE

THE LECTURES compiled in this volume were given by Rudolf Steiner in different European cities throughout the years 1912 and 1913. They deal with the experiences of the human soul after death and describe in detail how the living can relate themselves to the dead. Reading them, it becomes abundantly clear that excarnated souls need the spiritual support of those presently incarnated, and that those still on earth derive in turn enlightenment and support from their former earthly companions.

Today, with our mental capacities geared to dealing only with the sense perceptible world, any relationship to the dead becomes a difficult concept to grasp. Here in these lectures, however, the problem is presented like a theme with many variations. They continually bring back the same basic content and by allowing us to view it from every different angle, our understanding is awakened and direct spiritual intercourse with the dead gradually established.

Thus, in spite of what may appear on the surface to be mere repetition, the publication of this volume in its virtual entirety as it appeared in the German edition, is justified. Four lectures that were previously published in English translation are not included. They are *Links Between the*

Living and the Dead, two lectures, Rudolf Steiner Press, 1960, and *Occult Research into Life Between Death and a New Birth,* two lectures, Anthroposophic Press, 1949.

TABLE OF CONTENTS

INVESTIGATIONS INTO LIFE

BETWEEN DEATH AND REBIRTH

Milan, October 26–27, 1912

I

INVESTIGATIONS INTO LIFE
BETWEEN DEATH AND REBIRTH

Milan, October 26, 1912

IT WILL be my task here to explain to you some features of investigation of the spiritual world, and to indicate what the consequences of such knowledge are for life as a whole. He who has the task of communicating certain things to his fellowmen from the spiritual world cannot test too often their exactitude and absolute spiritual correctness. My aim is to impart something out of such verified knowledge in regard to the soul's life between death and a new birth. Lately, I have been able to test the research that can be made in this field. Particulars of these thorough investigations will be given in the second part of the lecture. This must be prefaced by some preliminary explanations pertaining to the attainment of spiritual knowledge.

A special disposition of the soul is necessary for the acquisition of spiritual knowledge, one to which the usual disposition in everyday life on the earthly plane is radically opposed. In external life, especially in our present day, the soul is in a continual state of unrest. Throughout the day the soul is constantly exposed to new impressions, and since it

3

identifies itself with these impressions it lives in a state of continuous restlessness.

The very opposite must take place if one would penetrate into the spiritual world. The first condition necessary for ascending into the spiritual world and for understanding the experiences gained in that realm is complete inner rest and steadiness of soul. This quietness of soul is more difficult to attain than we might think. All anxiety, all excitement and worry must cease in order to obtain inner calmness. In fact, during the time that we wish to lift ourselves into higher worlds all interests in outer life must be extinguished. We should be as if standing at one point, determined not to move, so that the events of the spiritual world may pass before us. In our everyday life on the physical plane we go from one thing to another while the things themselves remain stationary. This is not so in the spiritual world where we must bring things to us, to the point to which we are fixed, by means of our thinking activity. We must, as it were, go out of ourselves, penetrate the things and then bring them to us from outside. This may lead to alarming experiences for the soul.

We shall discover that during our normal life on earth we are able to change things, to correct what we have perceived or done wrongly. This is no longer so in the spiritual world. There we realize that things present themselves in a true or false aspect according to the condition we are in when entering the spiritual world. Therefore, all preparation for a correct insight into the spiritual world must take place before entering that realm because once we have passed the threshold we are no longer in a position to correct, but are forced to make the mistakes consistent with our own disposition of character. In order to avoid making certain mistakes

4

in the future, we must return to the physical plane, improve our disposition, and then return to the spiritual world to do better than previously. From this you will understand the importance of a sound and careful preparation before crossing the threshold into the spiritual world.

What I have said is closely connected with the present cycle of human evolution, but conditions for the soul were not always as they are today. In our time we should fear rather than welcome a too forcible appearance of a visionary world on entering the realm of the spirit. When we begin our exercises to rise into the higher worlds it is indeed possible for visionary experiences to penetrate into us. In our time there is only one safeguard against making mistakes in the presence of this visionary world, namely, to say to oneself that to begin with one can only learn certain things about oneself from these visions. The appearance of a whole host of visions around us need be nothing more than the mirroring of our own being. Our own disposition and maturity of soul, all we think and feel, transform themselves in the spiritual world into happenings that appear to be objective realities. For instance, when we see events in the astral world that seem objective to us, they may be nothing more than the reflection of our own virtues or defects, or indeed the effect of a headache. He who seeks genuine initiation, especially in our time, must endeavor to understand by thinking all that reaches him by way of the visionary experience. Therefore, the candidate for initiation will not rest until he has understood what he has encountered in the visionary world as thoroughly as he understands the physical world.

Now as we approach initiation our soul undergoes the same experiences as those during the period between death and a new birth. Recently in my occult research the following question arose. What is the relationship between the visionary world that one can find through initiation or as a result of a loosening of the ether body owing to shock, and the realm in which one dwells between death and a new birth? It was shown that when we turn our attention to the time between death and rebirth, we find, that is, setting aside the period of kamaloca, that we live in an objective world that can be compared to that of the initiate. This should not be taken, however, to mean that immediately after death we do not live in a real world. We live in an absolutely real world. We live there with those with whom we were connected on earth, and the connections are very real. But just as on earth we receive our perceptions by means of the senses, so after death we receive them by way of visions.

Let us consider the following instance. Suppose after death we meet someone in the spiritual world who died before us. He is there for us in reality, we stand before him, but we must be able to perceive him, must establish a relationship to him in the visionary world, just as in the physical world we would establish a connection with someone by means of our eyes and ears. Now, however, we encounter a difficulty that exists in the experience of the initiate and also in the life between death and rebirth. As previously explained, the world of visions presents at first only a reflection of ourselves. When a man meets us in the spiritual world a vision appears, but to begin with this vision only reflects the measure of affection or antipathy that we felt towards him on earth, or it reflects some other connection that we may have had with him in the past. We can therefore find ourselves in the presence of a person in the spiritual world and yet perceive nothing more than what was within our own soul before death. It may happen that we

6

meet a person in the spiritual world but remain cut off from him because of our feelings of affection or dislike that envelop us like a visionary cloud. Such meetings after death are accompanied by deep feeling, by a real inner experience, and this is most important. We might feel, for example, that we have not loved someone on earth as much as we should have done and now after death, notwithstanding that we are in his presence and wish to love him more, we find that we can only bring as much affection as we had for him on earth. This is true in spite of our earnest desire to love him more and make amends for what we failed to do on earth. We experience this sense of limitation, this total incapacity to develop further one's inner powers, as an immense weight on the soul after death.

This leads me to some of my recent research. The early experiences during the kamaloca period consist in essence of what the soul has received in its relations with its fellow men before death. After a certain time after death, for instance, we can no longer ask ourselves how we should love a person. We can then only ask ourselves how we loved him during earthly life, and as a result how we love him now. This condition gradually changes as after death we develop the faculty to sense the working of the beings of the spiritual world, of the Hierarchies, on the visions that surround us. Therefore, the situation that I have characterized is only altered as a result of a feeling that develops little by little. Beings of the Hierarchies are working on the mist that surrounds us; they shine upon this mist as the sun's rays irradiate the clouds. We have to take a certain number of memories of our life before death with us. They surround us like a cloud and on the basis of them we must develop the faculty to receive the light of the Hierarchies. Generally speaking, almost every soul in our time is prepared in this way to receive the influences of the higher Hierarchies. Today every person who dies and enters the spiritual world will reach the stage where the Hierarchies illumine the cloud of his visions.

The influence of the Hierarchies, this light-giving that occurs in the course of time, is also gradually altered. It changes in such a way that we experience little by little how this breaking-in of the light of higher Hierarchies could dim our consciousness. Then we become aware that the preservation of our consciousness depends upon certain specific things that happened before death. For instance, the consciousness of a person with an immoral soul disposition is more easily dimmed. It is therefore of the utmost importance that we cross the threshold of death with moral strength, for moral consciousness will keep our soul open to the light of the Hierarchies. Recently I have been able to examine the state after death of people with moral sentiments and also the state of those with an immoral disposition of soul, and in every case it could be established that a person with a moral disposition of soul was able to preserve clear, radiant consciousness after death, whereas those with an immoral soul constitution sink into a kind of dim twilight consciousness.

One might well ask what it matters if after death a person should fall into such a sleeping consciousness because then he would not suffer. He would even escape the consequences of his immorality. This argument will not hold because, with such a dimming of consciousness that is the result of immorality, the most terrible conditions of fear are connected. There is no greater fear after death than this darkening of consciousness.

8

Later, after a certain span of time has elapsed, one has quite other experiences. One compares, for instance, a variety of people during the period between death and rebirth, and one finds that during the later phase after death, in addition to the moral disposition the religious soul disposition plays a part. It is simply an unquestionable fact that souls deficient in religious thoughts experience a dimming of consciousness as a result of this deficiency. One cannot free oneself from the impression one gains in observing the state of men who have had only materialistic thoughts. Shortly after death their consciousness is dimmed, extinguished. This fact demonstrates that materialistic thoughts, however convincing they might appear to be, do not further human development after death.

I have thus described two phases of existence after death. In the first, one sees the effects of moral principles, in the second, the consequences of religious ideas. This is followed by a third period that would mean a dimming of consciousness for every soul were it not for certain cosmic measures that prevent this darkening. In investigating this third phase the total evolution of the whole of humanity through the various cycles of development will have to be considered. In pre-Christian times men could not acquire on earth what would have given them a consciousness in this third period after death. That they nevertheless had a consciousness during this third phase was due to the fact that since the beginning of earth evolution certain spiritual forces were bestowed on man that enabled him to preserve his consciousness. These forces, which were inherited by man from the beginning of the world, were preserved by the wise guidance of initiated leaders. We must bear in mind that in pre-Christian times all the various peoples

9

of the world received the influences of the Sanctuaries of Initiation, and there were many ways in which the spiritual life flowed forth from the Mysteries to the people.

These impulses became even weaker as human evolution approached the Mystery of Golgotha. An external proof of this can be seen in the advent of the great Buddha in pre-Christian times. A careful examination of the teachings of Buddha will not reveal any real information about the nature of the spiritual world. In fact, the spiritual world is characterized negatively in the teaching of Nirvana, and yet it is true that Buddha demanded of one who sought entry into the spiritual world that one should free oneself from all attachments to the physical world. But in the whole of Buddha's teachings we do not find any detailed description of the world of the spirit as we do, for instance, in the teachings of the Brahmans that still contain the traditions of ancient times. It must be emphasized that the facts referred to manifested themselves in various peoples until the time the Greeks experienced the meaning of the Mystery of Golgotha. Because during the early period of Greek civilization consciousness was dimmed between death and rebirth, the Greeks, who knew this, experienced the spiritual world as the realm of the shades. On earth man could create beauty, art, harmonious social conditions out of his own forces, but he was unable to acquire in the physical world what would give him a light during the third phase of life after death.

This is connected with the fact that in the Greek epoch mankind had reached the point in evolution when the ancient sources of tradition were exhausted. He could not procure by dint of his own powers in the physical world the forces needed after death to maintain the consciousness described. At this point in evolution mankind had to receive from without the impulse by means of which he could gain consciousness during this third phase. Man had lost the power of inheriting the consciousness between death and rebirth, but he could regain it by turning his thoughts to what had occurred at the Mystery of Golgotha. The matter stands as follows. What could be experienced during the Greek epoch through the Mystery of Golgotha has illumined men's consciousness in the third phase between death and rebirth. Understanding the Mystery of Golgotha is the impulse for consciousness in the third period after death.

If we now consider the Greco-Latin period, we can say that for the first phase after death the moral disposition of soul was the determining factor; for the second, the religious inclination; but for the third, the understanding of the Mystery of Golgotha was of prime importance. He who had not acquired this understanding suffered an extinction of consciousness in the third period after death, just as the Greeks experienced it previously. The Mystery of Golgotha signifies the re-enlivening of man's consciousness precisely during the middle period between death and rebirth. The ancient spiritual heritage that mankind had lost was restored to him through this event, and so the Christ event had to occur because of the conditions that prevailed in the lives of men. As evolution progressed mankind continually received new powers. During the first stage of Christian evolution it was the understanding of the Mystery of Golgotha as recounted by those who had lived at the time, and as transmitted by means of tradition, that gave the power to maintain consciousness in the third phase after death. Today, as a result of the further development of man's faculties, a new relation is again necessary, both to the Mystery of Golgotha and to the Christ being.

If we seek to understand the essence of the soul in our time, then we must realize that the deepest part of man's nature can penetrate today to a knowledge of the ego. Such a comprehension was not possible in former times. Among human beings at large we find this drawing-near to the ego in the grossest forms of egoism. It manifests itself in a wide variety of degrees until we reach the stage of the philosopher. In studying contemporary philosophy you will find that a secure standpoint is only reached when the human ego is spoken of. In pre-Christian times, when man attempted to gain knowledge of the world he turned his attention to outer phenomena; in other words, in order to philosophize he went out of himself. Today man looks inward, into himself, and only there, when he finds the ego, does he encounter a firm point of reference. I need only mention the great Fichte and the contemporary philosopher Bergson. Both agree that a man only finds a measure of inner peace if he discovers the ego. The reason for this lies in the fact that in earlier times humanity could not come out of its own powers to a knowledge of the ego. This experience was bestowed upon him during the Greco-Latin age through the Mystery of Golgotha. The Christ gave mankind the certainty that a spark of the divine dwells in the human soul. It continues to live in man, in him who has not only become flesh in a physical sense, but who has become flesh in a Christian sense, and that means to have become an "I." The possibility of recognizing the divine in a human individuality, namely, the Christ, is being ever more obscured in our time. This is due to the fact that the man of today penetrates increasingly into his personal ego and seeks to find the divine spark ever more in himself. We have seen that in the nineteenth century this way of viewing the ego was intensified to the point that the divinity of Christ was denied. The divine was understood merely as something abstract in the whole of mankind. So, for example, the German philosopher, David Friedrich Strauss, contended that one should not recognize one single historical Christ, but instead acknowledge the divine nature that animates the whole of humanity. Then the Resurrection signifies only what is manifested in all mankind as the awakening of the Divine Spirit.

This is the reason why the more man seeks the divine within himself, the more he will lose the understanding of the Mystery of Golgotha. The whole tendency of modern thinking is to seek the reflection of the divine exclusively in man. Because of this, ever greater obstacles prevent recognition that the Divine was incarnated within one personality. This has real consequences for the life between death and a new birth. If already in the Greco-Latin period man was not able by his own strength to maintain his consciousness in the third period after death, then it is all the more difficult in our time due to the general and philosophical egoism that prevails. In our present age, during the third phase after death the soul creates even greater obstacles for itself in its cloud of visions than during the Greco-Latin epoch.

If one considers the evolution of humanity in more recent times without prejudice, one must acknowledge that St. Paul said, "Not I, but the Christ in me." But modern man says, "I in me, and the Christ as far as I can admit Him. The Christ is only valid inasmuch as I can acknowledge Him through my own powers of reasoning."

In our present period there is only one way of maintaining a clear consciousness during the third phase after death, that is, by carrying certain memories from the previous life into our existence after death. In fact, during this period we would have to forget everything unless we were able to hold on to one particular recollection. If we have experienced on earth an understanding of Christ and the Mystery of Golgotha and have established a relationship to them, this will implant into us thoughts and forces that maintain our consciousness during this period after death. The facts clearly show that there is the possibility of remembering after death what had been understood on the earth in relation to the Mystery of Golgotha.

Once we have gained ideas and feelings about the Mystery of Golgotha, we shall be able to remember these after death, and also what is connected with them. In other words, after death we must carry our consciousness across an abyss, and this is done by means of the understanding of the Mystery of Golgotha that we have gained on earth. With this knowledge gained out of our memory during this period, we shall be able to cooperate in the correction of the faults that we bear in our soul as a result of our karma. If, however, we have not developed an understanding and deep realization of the words, "Not I, but the Christ in me," then our consciousness is extinguished and with it the possibility of improving our karma. Other powers must undertake the correction of our defects that ought to be corrected by us in accordance with our karma.

Naturally, every man returns through a new birth to earth, but it is of importance whether the consciousness has been extinguished or whether it has remained intact across the abyss. If we reach this period after death with a knowledge of the Mystery of Golgotha, we are able to look backward and remember that with all that is essentially human in us, we have come from God. We also experience that we have been able to save our consciousness because of our understanding of the Mystery of Golgotha, and that we can develop our consciousness further as we behold this Spirit now drawing near to us. Then we reach a point during this third phase after death when we can remember and say to ourselves that we are born out of the Spirit, *ex Deo nascimur*. One who has reached a certain stage of initiation never experiences the truth of the words, "I am born out of the Divine Spirit," as powerfully as when he transposes himself to this particular point. At this moment every soul who has developed an understanding of the Mystery of Golgotha experiences it. The significance of the words, *ex Deo nascimur*, is realized when one knows that their full depth will only be experienced when the soul has reached the middle period between death and rebirth.

When one knows these facts objectively, one would wish that more people in our time knew that the essence of these words can only be understood as characterized above. This saying has been made into a motto within our spiritual-rosicrucian movement precisely in order to awaken what should live within the soul between death and a new birth.

It would not be difficult to interpret this explanation as a preconceived opinion in favor of the Christian way of life. If this were the case, such a view would be entirely unanthroposophical. Spiritual science takes an objective position towards all religious creeds and studies them with equal interest. The facts that have been given here about the importance of the Mystery of Golgotha have nothing whatever to do with any form of denominational Christianity. They are simply objective occult realities. Yet the accusation has been levied against our Western spiritual movement that we speak out of a marked preference for Christianity as compared with other religions. Here, however, the Mystery of Golgotha is treated in the same way as any tangible fact in natural science. To say that the Mystery of Golgotha ought not be placed as a unique event in the evolution of humanity because other religions would not be able to acknowledge this fact shows complete misunderstanding. Let us consider the following. Today we have the sacred religious books of India and a modern Western world-conception. Today in the West we teach the Copernican system, and no one would suggest that we ought not to teach the Copernican theory because it is not contained in the sacred books of India! For the same reason no one can object to the teaching of the Mystery of Golgotha because it is not to be found in the religious writings of the ancient Hindus.

From this we see how unfounded is the reproach that the explanations here given about the Mystery of Golgotha come from a preference for Christianity. We are concerned with objective facts, and if you should ask why I will never modify in the slightest the importance attached to the Mystery of Golgotha, then the above reasons will provide the answer.

We do not study spiritual science for the sake of curiosity, nor from an abstract desire for knowledge, but in order to provide the soul with a necessary form of nourishment. By means of an understanding of the Mystery of Golgotha, we give the soul the possibility of developing those feelings that it will need in order to cross the abyss between death and rebirth as just described. One who has

16

understood that the soul after death can suffer a loss of consciousness, so heavy to bear in all future cycles of time, will seek every opportunity to bring the Mystery of Golgotha to the understanding of his fellow men.

For this reason the understanding of the Mystery of Golgotha is one of the most important facts that we must learn through the study of spiritual science.

The more progress we make in our present epoch, the more will the various religions be obliged to accept the facts we have presented today. The time will come when the followers of the Chinese, Buddhist and Brahman religions will find that it is no more contrary to their religion to accept the Mystery of Golgotha than it is to accept the system of Copernicus. In the future it will be considered a kind of religious egotism if this fact is not admitted by religions that are not Christian.

You will notice that in our considerations we have reached the Mystery of Golgotha although our starting point was the conditions between death and rebirth. One can give but a few indications in relation to an area such as we have dealt with here, but I wished at least to impart to you some of the results of my most recent research.

As the next lecture will be related to the present one, we probably will make a brief review of what has been said here, and then pass on to further considerations.

II

INVESTIGATIONS INTO LIFE
BETWEEN DEATH AND REBIRTH

Milan, October 27, 1912

OUR CONSIDERATIONS have led us to the point where consciousness after death can only be maintained by remembering the Mystery of Golgotha. Until this moment existence after death consists of recollections of life on earth by means of visions, not through the senses. During this period also, the realities of the spiritual world can only be perceived through visions.

Gradually the soul finds it more and more difficult to retain the memories of earthly life and a condition of forgetting sets in. If after death one meets a person one has known, one will at first readily recognize him. As time goes on this becomes more difficult, and later the connection can only be recalled by relating oneself to the Mystery of Golgotha. The more one is permeated by it, the easier it is to recognize one's surroundings. On reaching the stage where the recollections of the Mystery of Golgotha is needed in order to maintain consciousness, however, a great transformation begins. We are then no longer able to hold the previous visions. For example, until this phase we can speak in terms of astral color phenomena in this realm and

18

of the visionary images of beings surrounding us. Midway between death and a new birth visions and recollections fall away, we lose our connection with them, and they separate themselves off from our being. To characterize this phase more accurately let us consider the following, which upon first hearing might be quite shocking.

At this stage one feels oneself drawing away from the earth. The earth is far away below one, and journeying into the spirit world one feels that one has reached the Sun. Just as during earthly life we feel ourselves linked to the earth, so now we feel at one with the Sun with its whole planetary system. That is why in our modern occultism such stress is laid upon understanding how Christ came to earth from the Sun sphere. It is essential to grasp how Christ leads us to the Sun through the Mystery of Golgotha. Occultism shows that Christ is a Sun Being who leads us back to the Sun. Now comes what may cause a shock. It is imperative not only to understand our relationship to the Christ. We must grasp something further. The time now comes that we confront, and need to understand, the being known as Lucifer. The sensation in the Sun is not one of being surrounded by streaming physical light, but of dwelling in the pure light of the spirit. From this moment onward one experiences Lucifer no longer as an antagonistic being. On the contrary, he appears more and more to be fully justified in the world. One now senses the urge, in the further course of the life after death, to recognize Christ and Lucifer side by side as equally justifiable powers. However strange the equal importance of Christ and Lucifer may appear, this insight is reached from this stage onward and one comes to see these two powers more or less as brothers. The explanation for this is to be sought in experiences that the soul has to undergo in the further course of life after death.

I have often described the conditions of life on Saturn, Sun and Moon, and in them you have the spiritual path covered after death. The remarkable thing is that one does not experience the events in the order of cosmic creation: Saturn, Sun and Moon, but first comes the Moon-existence, then the Sun-existence and finally the Saturn-existence. When you read the descriptions I have given in *Cosmic Memory* and then proceed farther back from the Moon, you find the realm that the soul experiences on its backward journey after death. Beholding this directly in the spiritual world gives the impression of a recollection of life before birth. In the realm just characterized the moral element is of even greater importance for the further course of life. In *Cosmic Memory,* the "Akasha Chronicle," we described how one loses interest, which up to this stage was very strong, in all earthly experience. Our interest in men with whom we have been connected wanes, and we lose interest in things. We realize that the recollections we still have at this point are carried forward only by the Christ. Christ accompanies us, and as a result we are capable of remembering. If Christ were not to accompany us, our recollection of earthly life would vanish because it is the experience of uniting ourselves with Christ that beyond this point connects us with the earth.

So through a further stage in the spiritual world we gain a totally new interest in Lucifer and his realm. Severed from earthly interests, we can now experience the confrontation of Lucifer absolutely without danger. We make the remarkable discovery that Lucifer's influence is harmful to us only when we are entangled in earthly affairs. He now ap-

20

pears as the being who illumines what we have to undergo later in the world of the spirit. For a long span of time we feel that we must acquire what Lucifer can bestow upon us in these realms of the spirit world.

Again it may be a shock to speak of what is experienced only subjectively. Yet what appears shocking is perhaps in this case the most readily understandable, namely, that after awhile we become inhabitants of Mars. After we have felt ourselves to be Sun dwellers, having left the earth behind us, we now leave the Sun sphere and experience ourselves in our cosmic reality as inhabitants of Mars. In fact, for this phase it appears as if Christ had given us everything relating to the past and that Lucifer prepares us for our future incarnation. If this Mars sphere is experienced consciously and later on earth can be recalled by means of initiation, we discover that Lucifer bestows on us all experiences not originating in the earthly sphere that we carry within us through the width of the cosmos. Lucifer gives us everything unrelated to the earth. Our former human interest becomes more and more cosmic. Whereas previously we absorbed on earth what the mineral, the plant, the animal, air and water, mountain and valley gave us, we gather from this point onward the experiences that reach us from the cosmos. It is a form of perception that has always been known, but little understood, as the harmony of the spheres. We perceive everything as sounding forth out of cosmic surroundings: A world of harmonies rather than the separate sounds of the physical world.

At a certain point we experience ourselves as at the center of the universe. From all sides we perceive cosmic facts through the harmony of the spheres. We now leave the realm of Mars, and the occultist denotes the next sphere as that of Jupiter. As we proceed the harmony of the spheres increases in volume. Finally it is so powerful that we are numbed by it. Stupefied, we live into the harmony of the spheres.

After we have gone through the Jupiter sphere our existence reaches Saturn, the outermost limit of the solar system. At this juncture we undergo an important experience of a moral nature. If Christ has preserved our memory of earlier conditions on earth and protected us from the states of fear arising out of a waning consciousness, we realize, particularly in our present soul configuration, how little our life on earth was attuned to higher moral demands, to the majesty of the entire cosmic existence. Our past earthly life rises up reproachfully. Out of an undifferentiated darkness, and this is of the greatest importance, the sum total of the last incarnation as it formed itself karmically during that life, appears before the soul.

In fact, the overall picture of your present incarnation corresponds to what now arises in your soul at this stage after death, but everything you have to object to in your own last incarnation is poignantly experienced. We behold our last earthly life from a cosmic viewpoint.

From this time onward neither the Christ principle nor Lucifer can maintain our consciousness. Unless an initiation took place in a previous earth life, consciousness is definitely dimmed. It marks a necessary spiritual sleep-like condition following the consciousness that prevailed until then. This spiritual sleep is connected with another factor. Because all feelings and the capacity to form ideas have ceased, the total cosmic forces, with the exception of those emanating from the solar system, can now act directly upon man. Imagine the whole of the solar system out of action and only the forces outside it working. This will give you a picture of the influences that now begin to be operative.

Thus we have reached the point where we began our consideration yesterday.

Let us now consider the important relationship between the second phase of life after death and the embryonic period. You know that embryonic life begins with a small spherical germ. Occultly, we make the remarkable observation that in its earliest stages the embryo represents a mirror-picture of all the human being experiences out of the cosmos. This has been described above. At the outset the human germ carries a mirror-picture of cosmic existence from which its life in the solar system is excluded. It is remarkable that during the further stages of embryonic development all cosmic influences are rejected except those emanating from the solar system. These are absorbed by the embryo. Hereditary forces commence their activity on the embryo at a comparatively later stage when, during life after death, we have retraced our steps via Saturn, Jupiter and Mars. Therefore it may be said that the germ is already prepared by man during cosmic existence in a condition of universal sleep and before the embryonic period.

Let us now consider the stages in embryonic development that take place during the period of cosmic, universal sleep. In the diagram let us indicate one after another the

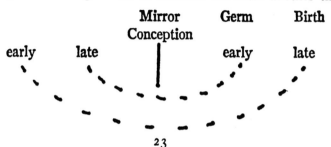

Mirror   Germ   Birth
Conception

early   late   early   late

23

prenatal conditions of the human being of the germ. Here we have a mirror-image.

Then the later embryonic conditions find their mirror-image in the early phase of prenatal life, and the early conditions of embryonic existence find their reflection in a later phase before conception. So we obtain a spiritual mirror-picture in reverse of embryonic development. Here is the embryo in the one direction, and for each phase in the one direction I find a mirror-image in the other. The two sides are related as object and mirror-image, and conception marks the point at which the mirror-images arise. If I were to represent embryonic development now, it would have to be drawn small. But its mirror-picture in the other direction would have to be much enlarged because what the human being undergoes in ten lunar months before birth is experienced in its reflection in a matter of years. Now take all that man experiences in the spiritual world until his reincarnation. In the first phase of his life after death he takes into himself the after-effects of his life on earth. During the second stage he gathers experiences out of the cosmos.

Life between death and a new birth is full of content, but one thing is missing. We do in fact recapitulate everything we have experienced from the previous incarnation until the present one. We sense cosmic being, but during the first stage of life after death we do not experience what has happened on the earth between the two incarnations. Until we reach the Sun sphere we are so preoccupied with our memories of life before death that our interest in events on the earth is completely diverted. We live with those individuals who also are dwelling in the spiritual world after death. We are fully involved in the relationships that we had with them on earth and shape these connections to fit their ultimate consequences. During this period our interest is continually diverted and thereby lessened for those who are still on the earth. Only when those who remain on earth seek us with their souls can a link with them be created. This should be considered an important moral element that throws light upon the connection between the living and the dead. A person who has died before us and whom we completely forget, finds it difficult to reach us here in earthly life. The love, the constant sympathy we feel for the dead, creates a path on which a connection with earthly life is established. During the early stages after death those who have passed on can live with us only out of this connection. It is surprising to what extent the cult of the commemoration of the dead is confirmed in its deeper significance by occultism. Those who have passed on can reach us most easily if they can find thoughts and feelings directed toward them from the earth.

The situation is different for the second stage between death and a new birth. We are then so deeply involved in cosmic interests that it becomes exceedingly difficult to establish a connection with the earth during this second period. Apart from the interest we take in the cosmos, we wish to cooperate in the right shaping of our further karma. In addition to our cosmic impressions we retain best what we have to correct karmically, and we help to shape a next life that will help to compensate for the karmic debts incurred.

Many people say that they cannot believe in reincarnation because they do not wish to return to a life on earth. This, for instance, is a current objection. I do not wish in the least to come back to the earth. Many say this. The above consideration regarding the period between death and rebirth corrects this view. During this period we want to return to life with all our strength in order to correct our karma. We forget all too easily after the cosmic sleep described, when we awaken into the present, that we actually wanted to reincarnate. It is immaterial whether it is our wish during life on earth to incarnate again. What matters is that we will it in the period between death and rebirth, and there we positively do. In many respects life between death and rebirth is the very opposite of what we experience here on earth between birth and death. Just as we are strengthened through sleep in earthly life and endowed with new forces, so as a result of the described cosmic sleep are we equipped with forces for our new incarnation.

Another question can be answered by these considerations. It is often asked, "If he incarnates so frequently, why must the human being begin over and over from infancy? Why does he not come into the world already equipped with everything he has to learn during childhood?" The answer lies in the fact that we do not experience what has happened on earth between our incarnations. For example, if a person was last incarnated on earth prior to the discovery of printing and incarnates again today, he will not have experienced what has developed in the intervening period. In fact, if one investigates the matter more closely from a cultural-historical aspect, one will find that in each incarnation one has to learn as a child what has happened on the earth in the intervening period. Consider, for instance, what a child of six had to learn in Roman times. That was quite different from what he has to learn today. The time span between two incarnations corresponds to the period needed for the cultural life on earth

26

to have changed completely. We do not return to an incarnation until the conditions on the earth have changed so that there is virtually no similarity to the conditions of our previous incarnation.

What I have described refers to the average person. For example, in one case consciousness after death might be dimmed earlier than in another, or the condition of sleep might set in more quickly, as you will have understood from what was said previously. But a cosmic law operates so that the cosmic sleep shortens the period that we spend in the spiritual world after death. The one who enters the condition of unconsciousness earlier experiences it more rapidly. Time passes at a quicker rate for him than for one whose consciousness extends farther. Investigations of life between death and rebirth do indeed reveal that unspiritual people reincarnate relatively more quickly than others. A person who only indulges in sensual pleasures and passions, who lives strongly in what we might call his animal nature, will spend but a short time between incarnations. This is due to the fact that such a person will fall comparatively rapidly into a condition of unconsciousness, of sleep. Hence he will travel quickly between the period of death and rebirth.

Moreover, I have only described an average case because I have specially considered people who reach a normal age in life. Fundamentally, there is a considerable difference between souls who die after their thirty-fifth year and those who die earlier. Only those who have reached their thirty-fifth year experience more or less consciously the various phases described. An early death brings about a more rapid condition of sleep between death and rebirth. It might be objected that, after all, one cannot be responsible for an early death and therefore one is innocently involved in an earlier cosmic sleep. Yet this objection is not valid. It is not so because an early death has been prepared as a result of previous karmic causes, and further development can take place just because the soul enters more rapidly into the cosmic realm. However strange and shocking this may appear, we know, as a result of objective investigations of cosmic existence, that man from a certain point onward expands into the cosmos and receives the impressions of the cosmos, of the macrocosmos. Just as man is most deeply involved in earthly matters during the middle years of his physical life, so in the middle period between death and rebirth he is most deeply involved in the cosmos.

Let us consider the child. As yet he does not live fully on the earth. He lives with all the inheritance from earlier periods, and he has to establish himself in earthly existence. Now consider the life of man after death. He lives with what he has carried away from the earth, and he has to acquire the perceptive faculties for life in the cosmos. In the middle period of our earthly existence we are most deeply entangled in earthly conditions, whereas in the middle stage between death and rebirth we are most deeply involved in cosmic conditions. The nearer we draw to the end of our existence on earth, the more we withdraw from earthly conditions in a physical sense. The farther we have gone beyond the mid-point between death and a new birth, the more we withdraw from the cosmos and turn again to the life on earth.

What I have just described as an analogy is not the basis of spiritual scientific investigations. An analogy of this kind occurs to an occultist only after he has made the necessary occult investigations and proceeds to compare the facts

28

available. Such an analogy also contains an error. Suppose we referred to the first period after death as that of childhood, and the second period as that of old age. We would make a mistake. During spirit-existence between death and a new birth we are in fact old to begin with, and we become children in relation to the spiritual life during the second period. Spiritual life flows in the reverse order. To begin with, we carry the errors and shortcomings of earthly life into the spiritual world. Then gradually during cosmic existence they are removed.

I was most surprised to find in ancient traditions not exactly a confirmation, but an indication regarding these facts. On earth during our physical existence we speak of getting old. In the spiritual world between death and rebirth we must say quite literally that we grow young. In fact, as far as his spirit-being is concerned, when someone is born in a particular place we can say that he became young there.

Now strangely enough, in the second part of *Faust* we find the words, "He became young in the Land of the Mists." Why does Goethe make use of the expression, "To become young" in order to express physical birth? When we go back into the past we find that a tradition prevailed in humanity that expresses the idea that at spiritual birth one becomes young. In fact, the more we look into past evolution, the more we encounter conditions of clairvoyance, as is continually stressed in our occultism. We find confirmation of them everywhere.

Consider, for instance, what was mentioned yesterday. From the moment of death we gradually free ourselves from earthly conditions, but during life between death and rebirth we live fully within cosmic conditions. These we experience as visions; they appear instead of sense impressions. I explained how the light of the Hierarchies falls on what we experience. We can characterize this situation as follows. Imagine that you did not have your consciousness *inside you,* but outside in your surroundings. You would not have the feeling that you were living in your body, but outside it. From outside you would feel that that is my eye, my nose, my leg. Then you would have to refer what you experience outside in the spirit to yourself. You would also have to refer the being of God to yourself, to let it be reflected in you. Such a stage arises after death when gazing back on man. The surroundings are reflected in him, even the Godhead.

Would it be too daring to accept the statement of a poet who said that life after death is the reflection of the divine? It is well known that Dante said that during one's existence in the spiritual world a point comes where one beholds the divine as man. Such an indication may appear unjustified. It may even seem playful, but one who is able to look into the deeper secrets of humanity will not take this view. In great poets we find again and again echoes of former conditions of clairvoyant knowledge, and by means of initiation such after-effects are revivified and lifted to human consciousness.

I have given you a few results of recent research into the conditions of life between death and a new birth, and I hope there will be another opportunity in the not too distant future to speak further on this theme.

MAN'S JOURNEY THROUGH THE PLANETARY

SPHERES AND THE SIGNIFICANCE OF A

KNOWLEDGE OF CHRIST

Hanover, November 18, 1912

III

MAN'S JOURNEY THROUGH THE PLANETARY SPHERES AND THE SIGNIFICANCE OF A KNOWLEDGE OF CHRIST

Hanover, November 18, 1912

W E SHALL begin this study by considering what we call human consciousness. What is human consciousness? In the first place, we can say that in the sleeping state— from the time of going to sleep in the evening until waking next morning—we have no consciousness. Nobody in possession of his five senses, however, doubts that he exists when he goes to sleep and loses consciousness. If he had any such doubt he would be holding the utterly senseless view that during sleep everything he experiences perishes and must come into being anew the next morning. Anyone who does not hold this senseless view is convinced that his existence continues during sleep. All the same, he has no consciousness.

During sleep we have no mental pictures, ideas, desires, impulses, passions, no pain or suffering—for if pain becomes so intense that sleep is prevented, it stands to reason that consciousness is present. Anyone who can distinguish between sleeping and waking can also understand what consciousness is. Consciousness is what enters a man's soul again every morning when he wakes from sleep. Ideas, mental pictures, emotions, passions, sufferings and so on—all this enters again into the soul in the morning. Now what is it that specially characterizes the consciousness of man? It is the fact that everything a man can have in his consciousness is accompanied by the experience of the "I." No mental image of which you could not think, *I* picture this to myself; no feeling of which you could not say, *I* feel; no pain of which you could not say, *I* suffer, would be a genuine experience of your soul. Everything you experience must be linked, and indeed it is, with the concept "I." Yet you are aware that this link with the concept "I" only begins at a certain age in life. At about the age of three, when a child begins to have this experience, he no longer says, "Carl speaks," or "Mary speaks," but "I speak." Knowledge of the "I" therefore is kindled for the first time during childhood. Now let us ask, "How does knowledge of the 'I' gradually awaken in the child?"

This question shows that apparently simple things are not so easily answered, although the answer may seem to lie very near at hand. How does the child pass out of the ego-filled ideas and mental pictures? Anyone who genuinely studies the life of childhood can understand how this happens. A simple observation can convince everyone how ego-consciousness develops and becomes strong in a child. Suppose he knocks his head against the corner of a table. If you observe closely you will find that the feeling of "I" is intensified after such a thing happens. In other words, the child becomes aware of himself, is brought nearer to a knowledge of self. Of course, it need not always amount to an actual injury or scratch. Even when the child puts

34

his hand on something there is an impact on a small scale that makes him aware of himself. You will have to conclude that a child would never develop ego-consciousness if resistance from the world outside did not make him aware of himself. The fact that there is a world external to himself makes possible the unfolding of ego-consciousness, the consciousness of the "I."

At a certain point in his life this consciousness of the "I" dawns in the child, but what has been going on up to this point does not come to an end. It is simply that the process is reversed. The child has developed ego-consciousness by becoming aware that there are objects outside himself. In other words, he separates himself from them. Once this ego-consciousness has developed it continues to come in contact with things. Indeed it must do so perpetually. Where do the impacts take place? An entity that contacts nothing can have no knowledge of itself, not, at least, in the world in which we live! The fact is that· from the moment ego-consciousness arises, the "I" impacts its own inner corporeality, begins to impact its own body inwardly. To picture this you need only think of a child waking up every morning. The ego and the astral body pass into the physical and etheric bodies and the ego impacts them. Now even if you only dip your hand in water and move it along, there is resistance wherever your hand is in contact with the water. It is the same when the ego dives down in the morning and finds its own inner life playing around it. During the whole of life the ego is within the physical and etheric bodies and impacts them on all sides, just as when you splash your hand in water you become aware of your hand on all sides. When the ego plunges down into the etheric body and the physical body it comes up against resistance everywhere, and this continues through the whole of life. Throughout his life the man must plunge down into his physical and etheric bodies every time he wakes. Because of this, continual impacts take place between the physical and etheric bodies on the one side and the ego and astral body on the other. The consequence is that the entities involved in the impact are worn away— ego and astral body on the one side, physical and etheric bodies on the other. Exactly the same thing happens as when there is continual pressure between two objects. They wear each other away. This is the process of aging, of becoming worn out, that sets in during the course of man's life, and it is also the reason why he dies as a physical being.

Just think of it. If we had no physical body, no etheric body, we could not maintain our ego-consciousness. True, we might be able to unfold such consciousness, but we could not maintain it. To do this we must always be impacting our own inner constitution. The consequence of this is the extraordinarily important fact that the development of our ego is made possible by destroying our own being. If there were no impact between the members of our being, we could have no ego-consciousness. When the question is asked, "What is the purpose of destruction, of aging, of death?" the answer must be that it is in order that man may evolve that ego-consciousness may develop to further stages. If we could not die, that is the radical form of the process, we could not be truly "man."

If we ponder deeply about the implications of this, occultism can give us the following answer. To live as men we need physical body, etheric body, astral body and ego. In human life as it is at present, we need these four members. But if we are to attain ego-consciousness, we must destroy them. We must acquire these members time and time again and then destroy them. Hence many earthly lives are necessary in order to make it possible for human bodies to be destroyed again and again. Thereby we are enabled to develop to further stages as conscious human beings.

Now in our life on earth there is only one member of our being whose development we can work at in the real sense, and that is our ego. What does it mean to work at the development of the "I?" To answer this question we must realize what it is that makes this work necessary. Suppose a man goes to another and says to him, "You are wicked." If this is not the case the man has told an untruth. What is the consequence of the ego's having uttered an untruth such as this? The consequence is that from this moment the worth of the ego is less than it was before the utterance was made. That is the objective consequence of the immoral deed. Before uttering an untruth our worth is greater than it is afterwards. For all time to come and in all spheres, for all eternity the worth of our ego is less as the result of such a deed. But during the life between birth and death a certain means is at our disposal. We can always make amends for having lessened the worth of our ego; we can invalidate the untruth. To the one we have called wicked we can confess, "I erred; what I said is not true," and so on. In doing this we restore worth to our ego and compensate for the harm done. In the case where our ego is involved it is still within our power during life to make the necessary adjustment. If, for example, we ought to have acquired knowledge of something but have forgotten all about it, our ego has lost worth, but if we make efforts we can recall it to memory and thus compensate for the harm done. To sum up, we can lessen the worth of our ego but we can also augment it. This faculty to correct a member of our being, to rectify its errors in such a way as to further its development, we possess in respect of the ego.

Man's consciousness does not, however, extend directly to his astral and etheric nature, and it extends far less to his physical nature. Although perpetual destruction of these members is taking place through the whole course of life, we do not know how to rectify it. Man has the power to repair the harm done to the ego, to adjust a moral defect or a defect of memory, but he has no power over what is continually being destroyed in his astral, etheric and physical bodies. These three bodies are being impaired all the time, and as we live on constant attacks are being made upon them. We work at the development of the ego, for if we did not do so during the whole of life between birth and death, no progress would be made. We cannot work as consciously at the development of our astral, etheric or physical body as we work at the development of our ego. Yet what is all the time being destroyed in those three bodies must be made good. In the time between death and a new birth we must again acquire in the right form—as astral body, etheric body and physical body—what we have destroyed. It must be possible during this time for what was previously destroyed to be repaired. This can only happen if something beyond our own power works upon us. It is quite obvious that if we do not possess magical powers it will not be possible for us to procure an astral body when we are dead. The astral body must be created for us out of the Great World, the Macrocosm.

We can now understand the question, "Where is the destruction we have caused in our astral body repaired?" We need a proper body when we are born again into a new bodily existence. Where are the forces that repair the astral body to be found in the universe? We might look for these forces on the earth with every kind of clairvoyance, yet we would never find them there. If it depended entirely on the earth, a man's astral body could never be repaired. The materialistic belief that all the conditions needed for human existence are to be found on the earth is utterly mistaken. Man's home is not only on the earth. True observation of the life between death and a new birth reveals that the forces man needs in order to repair the astral body lie in Mercury, Venus, Mars, Jupiter, Saturn, that is, in the stars belonging to the planetary system. The forces emanating from these heavenly bodies must all work at the repair of our astral body, and if we do not get the forces from there, we cannot have an astral body. What does that mean? It means that after death, and it is also the case in the process of initiation, we must go out of the physical body together with the forces of our astral body. This astral body expands into the universe. Whereas we are otherwise contracted into a small point in the universe, after death our whole being expands into it. Our life between death and new birth is nothing but a process of drawing from the stars the forces we need in order that the member we have destroyed during life can be restored. So it is from the stars that we actually receive the forces which repair our astral body.

In the domain of occultism—using the word in its true sense—investigation is difficult and full of complications. Suppose a man with good sight goes to some district in Switzerland, climbs a high mountain and then, when he has come down again, gives you an accurate description of what he has seen. You can well imagine that if he goes to the district again and climbs higher up the same mountain, he will describe what he has seen from a different vantage point. Through descriptions given from different vantage points it is obvious that an increasingly accurate and complete idea of the landscape will be obtained. Now people are apt to believe that if someone has become clairvoyant, he knows everything! It is by no means so. In the spiritual world, investigation always has to be gradual—"bit by bit," as it were. Even in respect to things that have been investigated with great exactitude, new discoveries can be made all the time. During the last two years it has been my task to investigate even more closely than before the conditions of life between death and rebirth, and I want to tell you now about the findings of this recent research.

You will of course realize that true understanding is possible only for those who can penetrate deeply into such a subject, those whose hearts and minds are ready for a study of this kind. In a single lecture it cannot be expected that everything will be proved and substantiated. If what has been said in the course of time is patiently compared and collated, it will be found that nowhere in the domain of the occultism studied here is there anything that does not fit in with the rest.

In the recent investigations of the life between death and a new birth the conditions prevailing during that period came very clearly to light. To the eyes of the spirit it is disclosed that the human being on the earth between birth and death, contracted as he is into the smallest possible space, emerges from it when he lays aside his physical body and expands farther and farther out into the universe. Having passed through the gate of death he grows stage by stage

40

out into the planetary spheres. First of all, he expands as far as the area marked by the orbit of the Moon; the sphere indicated by the position of the Moon then becomes his outermost boundary. When that point has been reached, kamaloca is at an end. Continuing to expand, he grows into the sphere formed by the orbit of Mercury, then into the sphere formed by the orbit of Venus. Then as his magnitude increases, his outermost boundary is marked by the apparent course of the Sun. We need not here concern ourselves with the Copernican theory of the universe. We need only picture the surrounding spheres as they were described in the Düsseldorf lectures on the *Spiritual Hierarchies*. Thus as man ascends into the spiritual worlds he expands into the planetary system, first into the sphere of the Moon, and ultimately into the outermost sphere, that of Saturn. All this is necessary in order that he shall come into contact with those forces needed for his astral body, which can be received only from the planetary system.

A difference becomes apparent when different individuals are observed. Suppose we observe a man after death whose bearing throughout life was morally good and who has therefore taken with him through the gate of death a moral disposition of soul. Such a man may be compared with another, for instance, who has taken with him through death a less moral tenor of soul. This makes a great difference, and it becomes evident when the men in question pass into the sphere of the forces of Mercury. What form does this difference take? With the means of perception at his disposal after the period of kamaloca is over, a man becomes aware of those who were near him in life and who predeceased him. Are these beings connected with him? True, he meets them all. He lives together with them after death,

41

but there is a difference in how he lives together with those with whom he was connected on earth. The difference is determined by whether the man brought with him through death a greater or lesser moral disposition of soul. If he lacked a moral sense in life, he does come together with members of his family and with his friends, but his own nature creates a kind of barrier that prevents him from reaching the other beings. A man with an immoral disposition becomes a hermit after death, an isolated being who always has a kind of barrier around him and cannot get through it to the other beings into whose sphere he has passed. But a soul with a moral disposition, a soul whose ideas are the outcome of purified will, becomes a sociable spirit and invariably finds the bridges and connections with the beings in whose sphere he is living. Whether we are isolated or sociable spirits is determined by our moral or immoral disposition of soul.

Now this has important consequences. A sociable spirit, one who is not enclosed in the shell of his own being, but can make contact with other beings in his sphere, is working fruitfully for the progress of evolution and of the whole world. An immoral man who after his death becomes a hermit, an isolated spirit, is working at the destruction of the world. He makes holes, as it were, in the texture of the universe commensurate with the degree of his immorality and consequent isolation. The effect of the immoral deeds of such a man is for him, torment; for the world, destruction.

A moral disposition of soul is therefore already of great significance shortly after the period of kamaloca. It also determines destiny for the next, the Venus period. A different category of ideas also comes into consideration then, ideas a man has evolved during life and that concern him when he enters the spiritual world. The ideas and conceptions are of a religious character. If religion has been a link between the transitory and the eternal, the life of soul in the Venus sphere after death is different from what it is if there has been no such link. Again, whether we are sociable or isolated, hermit-like spirits depends upon whether we were or were not of a religious turn of mind during life on earth. After death an irreligious soul feels as though enclosed in a capsule, a prison. True, such a soul is aware that there are beings around him, but he feels as though he were in a prison and unable to reach them. Thus, for example, the members of the Monistic Union, inasmuch as with their barren, materialistic ideas they have excluded all religious feeling, will not be united in a new community or union after death, but each of them will be confined in his own prison. Naturally, this is not meant as an attack upon the Monistic Union. It is merely a question of making a certain fact intelligible.

In the life on earth materialistic ideas are an error, a fallacy. In the realm of the spirit they are a reality. Ideas, which here in the physical world merely have the effect of making us shut ourselves off, incarcerate us in the realm of the spirit, make us prisoners of our own astrality. Through an immoral conception of life we deprive ourselves of forces of attraction in the Mercury sphere. Through an irreligious disposition of soul we deprive ourselves of forces of attraction in the Venus sphere. We cannot draw from this sphere the forces we need, which means that in the next incarnation we shall have an astral body that in a certain respect is imperfect.

Here you see how karma takes shape, the technique of forming karma. These findings of occult investigation throw remarkable light on an utterance Kant made as though instinctively. He said that the two things that inspired the greatest wonder in him were the starry heavens above and the moral law within. These are apparently two things, but in fact they are one and the same. Why does a feeling of grandeur, of reverent awe, come over us when we look up into the starry heavens? It is because without our knowing it the feeling of our soul's home awakens in us. The feeling awakens: Before you came down to earth to a new incarnation you yourself were in those stars, and out of the stars have come the highest forces that are within you. Your moral law was imparted to you when you were dwelling in this world of stars. When you practice self-knowledge you can behold what the starry heaven bestowed upon you between death and a new birth—the best and finest powers of your soul. What we behold in the starry heavens is the moral law that is given us from the spiritual worlds, for between death and a new birth we live in these starry heavens. A man who longs to discover the source of the highest qualities he possesses should contemplate the starry heavens with feelings such as these. To one who has no desire to ask anything, but lives his life in a state of dull apathy—to him the stars will tell nothing. But if one asks oneself, "How does there enter into me that which is never connected with my bodily senses?" and then raises his eyes to the starry heaven, he will be filled with the feeling of reverence and will know that this is the memory of man's eternal home. Between death and rebirth we actually live in the starry heavens.

We have asked how our astral body is built up anew in the spiritual world, and the same question can be asked about our etheric body. This body, too, we cannot help destroying

44

during our life, and again we must obtain from elsewhere the forces enabling us to build it up again, to make it fit to perform its work for the whole man during life.

There were long, long stretches of time in human evolution on earth when man was unable to contribute anything at all towards ensuring that his etheric body would be equipped with good forces in the next incarnation. Then man still had within him a heritage from times when his existence on earth began. As long as the ancient clairvoyance continued, there still remained in man forces that at death had not been used up, reserve forces, as it were, by means of which the etheric body could again be built up. But it lies in the very essence of human evolution that all forces eventually pass away and must be replaced by new ones. Today we have reached a point when man must do something himself in order that his etheric body may be built up again. Everything that we do as a result of our ordinary moral ideas, whatever response we make to a religion on the earth, limited as it may be to a particular people, with all this we pass into the planetary system and from there draw the forces for building up our astral body. There is only one sphere through which we pass without drawing from it these particular forces—the Sun sphere itself. For it is out of the Sun sphere that our etheric body must draw the forces enabling it to be built up again.

Conditions in pre-Christian times were such that as a man rose by stages into the spiritual world he took with him part of the forces of the etheric body, and these reserve forces enabled him to draw from the Sun what he needed for building his etheric body in a new incarnation. Today this has changed. It now happens more and more frequently that man remains unaffected by the forces of the Sun. If he fails to do what is necessary for his etheric body by filling his soul with a content that can draw from the Sun the forces required for the rebuilding of this etheric body, he passes through the Sun sphere without being affected by it.

Now the influence that can be felt to emanate from one particular religious denomination on earth can never impart to the soul what is necessary in order that existence may be possible in the Sun sphere. What we can instill into our etheric body, what we then need in order that the soul's sojourn in the Sun sphere may be fruitful—this can come only from the element that flows through all the religions of mankind in common. What is this? If you compare the different religions of the world—and it is one of the most important anthroposophical tasks to study the core of truth in the different religions—you will find that these religions were always right in their way, but right for a particular people, for a particular epoch. They imparted to this people, to this epoch, what it was essential for this people and epoch to receive. In point of fact we know most about those religions that were able to serve their particular time and people by clinging egoistically to the form in which they originally issued from the fount of religious life.

For more than ten years now we have been studying the religions, but it must be realized that once there had to be given to humanity an impulse transcending that of the single religions and embracing everything to which they had pointed. How did this come to be possible? It became possible through a religion in which there was no single trace of egoism. The supremacy of this religion lies in the fact that it did not limit itself to one people and one epoch. Hinduism, for instance, is an eminently egoistic religion,

46

for a man who is not a Hindu cannot be received into it. This religion is specially adapted for the Hindu people, and the same applies to the other territorial religions; their original greatness lay in the fact that they were adapted to particular earthly conditions. Those who do not admit that the religions were adapted to particular conditions, but maintain that all religious systems have emanated from one undifferentiated source, can never acquire real knowledge.

To speak only of unity amounts to saying that salt, pepper, paprika and sugar are on the table, but we are not concerned with each of them individually. What we are looking for is the unity that is expressed in these different substances. Of course, one can speak like this, but when it is a question of passing on to practical reality, of using each substance appropriately, the differences between them will certainly be apparent. Nobody who uses these substances will claim that there is no difference between them. If there is really no difference, then just put salt or pepper instead of sugar into your coffee or tea, and you will soon find out the truth! Those who make no real distinction between the several religions, but say that they all come from the same source, are making the same kind of blunder.

If we wish to know how a living thread runs through the different religions towards a great goal, we must seek to understand this thread, and study the value of each religion for its particular sphere. This is what we have been doing for the last ten years in our Middle-European Section of the Theosophical Society. A beginning has been made towards discovering the nature of a religion that has nothing to do with differences in humanity, but only with the essential human as such, without distinction of color, race, and

47

so forth. What form has this taken? Can it really be said that we have a "national" religion such as is found among the Hindus or the Jews? If we were to worship Wotan we should be in the same position as the Hindus. But we do not worship Wotan. The West has acknowledged the Christ, and Christ was not a Westerner, but an alien with respect to His lineage. The attitude to Christ that the West has adopted is not an egoistic or nationalistic adherence to a creed. The domain touched upon here cannot, of course, be exhaustively dealt with in a single lecture. It is only possible to speak of particular aspects, and one aspect is that the attitude adopted by the West to its professed religion has been absolutely unegoistical.

The supremacy of the Christ Principle is shown in another way, too. Think of a congress where learned representatives of the different religions have gathered with the aim of comparing the various systems of religion quite impartially. To such a congress I should like to put the question, "Is there any religion on the earth in which one and the same saying means something different when made from two different sides?" This is actually what occurs in Christianity. Christ Jesus speaks profound words in the Gospel when He says to those around Him, "In all of you there is Divinity; are you then not Gods?" He says with all power and authority, "Ye are gods!" (John 10, 34). Christ Jesus means by these words that in every human breast lies a spark that is Divine. This spark must be kindled in order that it may be possible to say, "Be as the gods." A different and indeed exactly opposite effect is the aim of words spoken by Lucifer when he approaches man in order to drag him down from the realm of the Gods, "Ye shall be as God" (Genesis 3, 5). The meaning here is entirely dif-

48

ferent. The same utterance is made at one time in order to corrupt humanity at the beginning of the descent into the abyss, and at another time as a pointer to the supreme goal!

Look for the same thing in any other denominational creed, and the one utterance or the other may be found, but never both. Close examination will show what depth of meaning lies in the few words that have just been spoken. The fact that these significant utterances have become an integral part of Christianity shows clearly that what is really important is not the mere content of the words, but the Being who utters them. Why is it so? It is because Christianity is working to achieve the fulfillment of the principle that gives expression to its very core, namely, that there is not only kinship among those related by physical descent, but among all mankind. There is something that holds good without distinction of race, nationality or creed, and reaches beyond all racial traits and all epochs of time. Christianity is so intimately connected with the soul of man because what it can bestow need not remain alien to any man. This is not yet admitted all over the earth, but what is true must ultimately prevail.

Men have not yet reached the stage of realizing that a Buddhist or a Hindu need not reject Christ. Just think what it would mean if some serious thinker were to say to us, "You who are followers of Christ ought not to maintain that all denominations and creeds can acknowledge Him as their supreme goal. In so doing you give preference to Christ, and you are not justified in making such a statement."

If this were said, we should have to answer, "Why are we not justified? Is it because a Hindu might also demand that veneration be paid only to his particular doctrines? We have no desire whatever to deprecate these doctrines; we honor them as highly as any Hindu. Would a Buddhist be justified in saying that he may not acknowledge Christ because nothing is said to this effect in His scriptures? Is anything essential at stake when a truth is not found in particular writings or scriptures? Would it be right for a Buddhist to say that it is against the principles of Buddhism to believe in the truth of the Copernican theory of the universe, for no mention of it is made in His books? What applies to the Copernican theory applies equally to the findings of modern spiritual-scientific research concerning the Christ-being, namely, that because He has nothing to do with any particular denomination, the Christ can be accepted by a Hindu or an adherent of any other religion. Those who reject what spiritual science has to say about the Christ impulse in relation to the religious denominations simply do not understand what the true attitude to religion should be."

Perhaps some day the time will come when it will be realized that what we have to say about the nature of the Christ impulse and its relation to all religious denominations and world-conceptions speaks directly to the heart and soul, as well as endeavoring to deal consistently with particular phases of the subject. It is not easy for everyone to realize what efforts are made to bring together things that can lead to the true understanding of the Christ impulse needed by man in the present cycle of his existence. Avowal of the belief in Christ has nothing fundamentally to do with any particular religion or religious system. A true Christian is simply one who is accustomed to regard every human being as bearing the Christ principle in himself, who looks for the Christ principle in a Chinese, a Hindu, or whoever he may be. In a man who avows his belief in Christ is founded the realization that the Christ impulse is not confined to one part of the earth. To imagine it as confined would be a complete fallacy. The reality is that since the Mystery of Golgotha, Paul's proclamation to the region with which he was connected has been true—Christ died also for the heathen. Humanity must learn to understand that Christ did not come for one particular people, one particular epoch, but for all the peoples of the earth, for *all* of them! Christ has sown His spirit-seed in every human soul, and progress consists in the souls of men becoming conscious of this.

In pursuing spiritual science we are not merely elaborating theories or amassing a few more concepts for our intellects, but we meet together in order that our hearts and souls may be affected. If in this way the light of understanding can be brought to bear upon the Christ impulse, this impulse itself will eventually enable all men on earth to realize the deep meaning of Christ's words, "When two or three are gathered together in My Name, there am I in the midst of them." Those who work together in this spirit find the bridge that leads from soul to soul. This is what the Christ impulse will achieve over the whole earth. The Christ impulse itself must constitute the very life of our groups.

Occultism reveals that if we feel something of the reality of the Christ impulse, a power has penetrated into our souls that enables them to find the path through the Sun sphere after death and makes it possible for us to receive a healthy etheric body in the next incarnation. We can only assimilate spiritual science in the right way by receiving the Christ impulse into ourselves with deep understanding. Only this will ensure that our etheric body will be strong and vigorous when we enter a new incarnation. Etheric bodies will deteriorate more and more if men remain in ignorance of Christ and His mission for the whole of earth evolution. Through understanding the Christ-being we shall prevent this deterioration of the etheric body and partake of the nature of the Sun. We shall become fit to receive forces from the sphere whence Christ came to the earth. Since the coming of Christ we can take with us from the earth the forces that lead us into the Sun sphere. Then we can return to the earth with forces that in the next incarnation will make our etheric body strong. If we do not receive the Christ impulse, our etheric body will become less and less capable of drawing from the Sun sphere the forces that build and sustain it, enabling it to work in the right way here on the earth. Earthly life is really not dependent upon theoretical understanding, but upon our being permeated through and through with the effects of the Event of Golgotha. This is what is revealed by genuine occult research.

Occult research also shows us how we can be prepared to receive the physical body. The physical body is bestowed upon us by the Father principle. It is through the Christ impulse that we are able to partake of the Father principle in the sense of the words, "I and my Father are one" (John 10, 30). The Christ impulse leads us to the divine powers of the Father.

What is the best result that can be achieved by spiritual deepening? One could imagine someone among you going out after the lecture and saying at the door, "I have forgotten every single word of it!" That would, of course, be an extreme case, but it would really not be the greatest calamity. For I could imagine that such a person does nevertheless take with him a feeling resulting from what he has heard here, even though he may have forgotten everything! It is this feeling in the soul that is important. When we are listening to the words we must surrender ourselves wholly in order that our souls shall be filled with the great impulse. When the spirit-knowledge we acquire contributes to the betterment of our souls, then we really have achieved something. Above all, when spiritual science helps us to understand our fellow men a little better, it has fulfilled its function, for spiritual science is life, immediate life. It is not refuted or confirmed by disputation or logic. It is put to the test and its value determined by life itself, and it will establish itself because it is able to find human beings into whose souls it is allowed to enter.

What could be more uplifting than to know that we can discover the fount of our life between death and rebirth. We can discover our kinship with the whole universe! What could give us greater strength for our duties in life than the knowledge that we bear within us the forces pouring in from the universe and must so prepare ourselves in life that these forces can become active in us when, between death and rebirth, we pass into the spheres of the planets and of the Sun. One who truly grasps what occultism can reveal to him about man's relation to the world of the stars can say with sincerity and understanding the prayer that might be worded somewhat as follows, "The more conscious I become that I am born out of the universe, the more deeply I feel the responsibility to develop in myself the forces given to me by a whole universe, the better human being I can become." One who knows how to say this prayer from

53

the depths of the soul may also hope that it will become in him a fulfilled ideal. He may hope that through the power of such a prayer he will indeed become a better and more perfect man. Thus what we receive through true spiritual science works into the most intimate depths of our being.

RECENT RESULTS OF OCCULT INVESTIGATION

INTO LIFE BETWEEN DEATH AND REBIRTH

Vienna, November 3, 1912

IV

RECENT RESULTS OF OCCULT INVESTIGATION
INTO LIFE BETWEEN DEATH AND REBIRTH

Vienna, November 3, 1912

IT AFFORDS me great pleasure to be with you this evening on the occasion of my presence here in Vienna, which was necessitated by certain other circumstances. As this is a special meeting, I would like to speak about more intimate matters that can only be dealt with in smaller groups long acquainted with spiritual science.

In occult research one cannot check often enough the facts one has repeatedly investigated, and about which one has spoken, for they are facts of the spiritual world that is not easily accessible and comprehensible to man. There is a constant danger of misinterpreting in one way or another, and events may be viewed incorrectly. This is the reason the results obtained must be checked again and again. The principal events of life in the spiritual world have, of course, been known for thousands of years, yet it is difficult to describe them. I am deeply grateful that recently I had the opportunity to concern myself more intimately again with an important aspect of occultism, namely, the realm of life between death and a new birth. It is not so much that new facts come to light, but that one has the possibility to present things in a more exact and accurate way. So today I would like to speak of the period that for supersensible perception is of the utmost importance, that is, the period between death and rebirth. I will not deal so much with the period immediately following death, the kamaloca period, descriptions of which cán be found in my writings, but with the succeeding period, the actual sojourn of man in the spiritual world between death and rebirth. This description will be prefaced briefly by the following remarks.

One learns to know the period between death and rebirth either by initiation or by going through the portal of death. Mostly one does not take sufficiently seriously the difference that exists between knowledge acquired in the sense world by means of our senses and intellect and knowledge acquired of the spiritual world, either through initiation in a physical body in this life or without this body when we have gone through the gate of death. In a sense, everything is reversed in the spiritual world. I will refer to two characteristics to show how fundamentally different are the spiritual world and the normal sense world.

Let us consider our existence in the sense world during waking consciousness from morning until night. The objects we perceive by means of our eyes and ears come to us. Only in the higher realms of life, so to speak, in the spheres of knowledge and art, do we have to exert ourselves to participate in drawing things towards us. Apart from this, in the rest of outer life everything from morning until night that impinges on our senses and our intellect is brought to us. Wherever we go, in the street, in the daily round of life, every moment is filled with impressions, and apart from the exceptions mentioned we make no effort to bring them about. They come about of their own accord.

It is different as regards what happens through us in the physical world. Here we have to be active, move from place to place, be on the go. It is an important characteristic of daily life that what is presented to our perception comes to us without our activity. However grotesque it may appear, the opposite is true in the spiritual world. There one cannot be active, one cannot draw anything towards one by moving from one place to another. Nor can one bring anything to one simply by moving a limb—by the movement of a hand, for example. Above all, for something to happen in the spiritual world it is essential that there be absolute calmness of soul.

The quieter we are, the more can happen through us in the spiritual world. We simply cannot say that anything happens in the spiritual world as a result of hurry and excitement. We need to develop loving participation in a mood of soul calmness for what is to happen, and then wait patiently to see how things come to pass. This calmness of soul, which in the spiritual world is creative, does not quite have its equal in ordinary physical life. It is similar on higher levels of earthly existence to the sphere of knowledge and of the arts. Here we have something analogous. The artist who cannot wait will not be able to create the highest he is capable of. For this, he needs patience and inner calmness of soul until the right moment dawns, until the intuition comes. One who seeks to create according to a schedule will produce only works of inferior quality. He who seeks to create, be it the smallest work, prompted by an outer stimulus will not succeed as well as if he had waited quietly with loving devotion for the moment of inspiration. We might say for the moment of grace. The same is true of the spiritual world. In it there is no rush and excitement but only calmness of soul.

Fundamentally, this must also be the way with the growth of our movement. Propaganda campaigns and a desire to force spiritual science on our fellow men are useless. It is best if we can wait until we meet those who inwardly need to hear about the spirit, who are drawn to it. We should not nurture longings to bring everyone to spiritual science. We shall find that the calmer we are, the more people will come to us, whereas forceful propaganda merely puts people off. Public lectures are held only in order that what has to be said should be said and those who wish to receive what is communicated can do so. Our attitude within our spiritual scientific movement must be a reflection of the spiritual so that what has to happen can happen and is awaited with inner silence.

Let us consider an initiate who knew that something was to happen at a particular time out of the spiritual world. I have often drawn attention to an important event that had its origin in the spiritual world but which does not yet reveal itself in a marked way. I refer to the year 1899, the end of the small Kali Yuga. That year brought a certain impulse that was to give mankind the possibility of an inner soul-awakening. In earlier times it was produced by external stimuli from the spiritual world, usually denoted as chance occurrences.

I would like to relate a particular instance. In the twelfth century there lived a certain personality named Norbert, who founded an order. At first he led a worldly, dissolute life. Then one day he was struck by lightning. Such events are by no means rare in history. A flash of lightning can have the effect of shaking up the physical and ether bodies. His whole life was changed. Here we have an example of how an outer happening is used by the spiritual world to alter the course of a man's life. Such chance phenomena are not uncommon. They completely shake up the connection between the physical and ether bodies and radically transform the individual concerned. That was the case in this instance. It is not a question of coincidence. Such events are carefully prepared in the spiritual world so as to bring about a change in a person. Since the year 1899, however, such happenings have taken on a more intimate character. They are less outward and the human soul is deepened more and more inwardly. In fact, in order to produce such a universal revolution as that of 1899, not only all the powers and beings of the spiritual world had to cooperate, but also the initiates who lived on earth. They do not say, "Prepare yourselves." They do not shout it in people's ears, but they act in such a way that the impulse comes from within so that people learn to understand it from within. Then people remain inwardly calm, concern themselves with such thoughts, allow them to work within the soul, and wait. The more quietly such thoughts are carried in the soul, the more strongly such spiritual events occur. The most important thing is to wait the moment of grace, to wait for what will happen to us in the spiritual world.

It is different in regard to the acquisition of knowledge in everyday life. Here we have to gather things together, to work and exert ourselves in order to obtain it. In the physical world the rose we find along the wayside gladdens us. This would not happen on the spiritual plane. There something similar to a rose would not appear unless we had exerted ourselves to enter a particular realm of the spirit in order to draw it towards us. In fact, what we have to do here to act, we do in the spiritual world in order to know, and what has to happen through us has to be awaited in stillness. Only the higher activities of man, where the spiritual world weaves into the physical, afford a reflection of the events in the spiritual world. That is why it is essential, if one wishes inwardly to understand what is imparted by spiritual science, to develop two qualities of soul. Firstly, love for the spiritual world, which leads to an active grasping of the spirit and is the surest way of enabling us to bring the things of the spirit towards us, and secondly, inner rest, a calmness of soul, a silence free from vanity or ambition anxious to attain results, but capable of receiving grace, able to await inspiration. In actual cases this patient expectation is not easy, but there is a thought that can help us to overcome obstacles. It is difficult to accept because it strikes so deeply against our vanity. This thought is that in the universal pattern it is of no importance whether something happens through us or through another person. This should not deter us from doing everything that has to be done. It should not prevent us from performing our duty, but it should keep us from hurrying to and fro. How glad every individual feels that *he* is capable, that *he* can do it. A certain resignation is necessary for us to feel equally glad when someone else can and does do something. One should not love something because one has done it oneself, but love it because it is in the world irrespective of whether he or someone else has done it. If we repeatedly ponder this thought it will lead most certainly to selflessness. Such moods of soul are essential to enter into the spiritual world, not only as an investigator but also to understand what has been discovered. These inner attitudes are far more important than visions, although they, too, have to be present. They are essential because they enable us to evaluate the visions rightly.

Visions! One need only mention the word and everybody knows what is meant by it. Actually, the whole of our life after death once kamaloca is over consists of visions. When the human being has gone through the gate of death and kamaloca and then enters the actual spiritual world, he lives in a realm in which it is as if he were surrounded from all sides by mere visions, but visions that are mirror-images of reality. In fact we can say that just as we perceive the physical world by means of colors that the eye conjures forth for us, and sounds mediated by the ear, we experience the spiritual world after death by means of visions in which we are enveloped.

Now, as I wish to speak more intimately of these things, I shall have to use a more descriptive form. Certain things may sound rather strange, but that is how they reveal themselves to genuine spiritual investigation.

The kamaloca period unfolds as I have described it in my book, *Theosophy,* but it can be characterized also in a different way. One may for instance ask, "When a person has gone through the gate of death, where does he feel himself to be?" One can answer this question by asking, "Where is man during his kamaloca period?" This can be expressed spatially in words that express our physical world. Imagine the space between the earth and the moon, the spherical space described when the orbit of the moon is taken as the outermost path away from the earth. Then you have the realm in which man, loosened from the earth, dwells during the kamaloca period.

It may sound strange, but when the kamaloca period has been completed, a human being leaves this sphere and enters the actual celestial world. Also in this connection, accurate and genuine investigation shows that things are reversed in relation to the physical plane. Here we are bound outwardly to the earth, surrounded by the physical world and separated from the heavenly spheres. After death the earth is separated from us and we are united with the heavenly spheres. As long as we dwell within the Moon sphere we are in kamaloca, which means that we are still longing to be connected with the earth. We proceed beyond it when we have learned through life in kamaloca to forego passions and longings. The sojourn in the spiritual world must be imagined quite differently from what is customary on earth. There we are spread out in space, we feel ourselves in the whole of space. That is why the experience, be it of an initiate or of a person after death, is one of feeling oneself spread out in space, expanding after death (or as an initiate) and being limited by the Moon orbit as by a skin. It is like this and it is of no avail to use words our contemporaries would more easily forgive because by doing so one would not express the facts more correctly. In public lectures such shocking things have to be left out, but for those who have concerned themselves with spiritual science for a longer time it is best to say things plainly.

After the life in kamaloca we grow further out into space. This will depend on certain qualities that we have acquired previously on the earth. A long span of our evolution after death, and our ability to expand to the next sphere, is determined by the moral attitude, the ethical concepts and feelings we developed on earth. A person who has developed qualities of compassion and love—qualities that are usually termed moral—lives into the next sphere so that he becomes acquainted with the beings of that sphere. A man who brings a lack of morality into this realm dwells in it like a hermit. It may be best characterized by saying that morality prepares us for living socially together in the spiritual world. We are condemned to a fearful loneliness, filled with a continual longing to get to know others without being able to do so, as a result of a lack of morality in the physical world of the heart as well as of the mind and will. Either as a hermit or as a sociable being who is a blessing in the spiritual world, do we dwell in this second sphere known in occultism as that of Mercury. Today in ordinary astronomy this is known as the Venus sphere. As has often been mentioned, the names have been reversed.

Now man's being expands up to the orbits of the morning and the evening stars, whereas previously it expanded only to the Moon. Something strange happens at this point. Until the Moon sphere we are still involved in earthly affairs, but even beyond, the connection with earthly matters is not entirely severed. We still know what we have done on the earth, what we have thought. Just as here we can remember, so we know there. But recollection may be painful! On earth if we have done a person some injustice or have not loved him as much as we should, we can make up for these feelings. We can go to him and put things right. This is no longer possible from the Mercury sphere onward. We behold the relationships in recollection. They remain but we cannot alter them.

Let us assume that a person has died before us. According to the earthly connection we should have loved him, but did not do so as much as we should have done. We meet him again since we were related to him previously because after death we do in fact encounter all the people with whom we were connected. To begin with, this cannot be altered. We reproach ourselves with not having loved him enough, but we are incapable of changing our soul-disposition so as to love him more. What has been established on the earth remains. We cannot alter it. These facts relating to the correct, unchangeable perception of love made a strong impression on me during my recent investigations this summer. Much comes to light that eludes most people. I wanted to convey this to you.

One learns to know these strange facts by means of spiritual cognition. One lives in the Mercury sphere in former relationships with people, and they cannot be altered. One looks back and unfolds what one has already developed.

Although I have concerned myself a great deal with Homer, yet a particular passage became fully clear only during recent occult investigations when the facts described came powerfully to me. It is the passage in which Homer calls the realm after death, "the land of the shades where nothing can change." It can be understood by the intellect but what the poet seeks to convey about the spiritual world, how he speaks as a prophet, that one only learns to know when the corresponding discovery has been made by means of spiritual research. This is true of every genuine artist. He need not understand with his everyday consciousness what comes to him in inspiration. What humanity has received through its artists in the course of centuries will not fade because of the spreading of our spiritual movement. On the contrary, art will be deepened and mankind will value all the more its true artist when, as a result of occult

66

investigation, the spiritual realm is reached—the realm out of which the artist has drawn his inspiration. Of course, those who at one time or another have been regarded as important artists but are not truly great will not be singled out. Passing greatness will be recognized for what it is. It contains no inspiration from the spiritual world.

The next sphere is termed the Venus sphere in occultism. We now expand our being up to Mercury, which is known as the occult Venus. In this sphere the human being again is strongly influenced by what he brings. He who has something to bring becomes a social being, and he who has nothing to give is condemned to loneliness. A lack of religious inclination is dreadfully painful. The more religious the disposition of soul we have acquired, the more social we become in this sphere. People who lack religious inclination cut themselves off. They cannot move beyond a sheath or shell that surrounds them. Nevertheless, we get to know friends who are hermits, but we cannot reach them. We continually feel as if we have to break through a shell but are incapable of doing so. In the Venus sphere, if we have no religious inwardness, it is as if we were to freeze up.

This is followed by a sphere in which, however strange it may appear, the human being, and this is so for everyone after death, expands up to the Sun. In the not too distant future different concepts will be held about the heavenly bodies from those adhered to by astronomy today. We are connected with the Sun. There is a period between death and rebirth when we become Sun beings. But now something further is necessary. In the first sphere we need moral inclination and in the Venus sphere, a religious life. In the Sun sphere it is essential that we truly know the nature and being of the Sun spirits and above all, the ruling Sun Spirit, the Christ, and that we made a connection with Him on earth.

When mankind still possessed an ancient clairvoyance, this, with the Christ connection, was established by living into the divine grace of the past. This has vanished and the Mystery of Golgotha, prepared by the Old Testament, was there to bring an understanding of the Sun Being to man. Since the Mystery of Golgotha mankind has naïvely endeavored to draw towards the Christ. Today this no longer suffices. In our time spiritual science must bring an understanding of the Sun Being to the world. It was clearly understood for the first time during the Middle Ages when the Grail Saga found its deeper origin in Europe. Through the understanding given by means of spiritual science what was brought by the lofty Sun Spirit, by the Christ, the Christ Who came down and through the Mystery of Golgotha has become the Spirit of the earth will be retrieved.

The impulse given by the Mystery of Golgotha is destined through spiritual science to unite all religious creeds in peace over the whole earth. It remains the basic challenge of spiritual science to treat all religions with equal attention without giving preference to any of them for outer reasons. Because we place the Mystery of Golgotha at the fulcrum of world evolution, our movement is accused of giving a preference to the Christian religion. Yet this accusation is quite unjustified. Let us understand how matters really stand with such accusations. If a Buddhist or Brahman were to accuse us of this we would say, "Is the only issue what is to be found in sacred writings? Providing one does not reject a religion, is what is not to be found in its books to the detriment of a religion? Cannot every Buddhist accept the Copernican system and yet remain a Buddhist?" To be able to do so is a sign of progress for humanity at large. So is the knowledge that the Mystery of Golgotha stands in the center of the evolution of the world, irrespective of whether it is mentioned in ancient writings or not.

If we understand the Mystery of Golgotha, and realize what happened there, then in the Sun sphere we become sociable spirits. As soon as we have gone beyond the Moon sphere, we are spiritually surrounded by visions. On encountering a deceased friend after death we meet him in the form of a vision, but he dwells in this reality. They are visions, nevertheless, built up on the basis of recollections of what we have done on earth.

Later, beyond the Moon sphere, this is still the case but now the spiritual beings of the higher hierarchies illumine us. It is as if the Sun rose and irradiated the clouds in the Sun sphere. Just as we only learn to know the spiritual hierarchies in the Mercury sphere if we have a religious inclination, so in the Sun sphere we must be permeated by a Jehovah-Christian mood of soul. The outer spiritual beings approach us. Again something remarkable occurs, confirmed by objective occult research. Beyond the Moon the human being is like a cloud woven out of spirit, and when he enters the Mercury sphere, he is illumined by spiritual beings. That is why the Greeks called Mercury the messenger of the Gods. In this sphere lofty spiritual beings illumine man. We gather mighty impressions when we unfold out of the realm of occult investigation what has been given to humanity in the form of art and mythology.

So, Christ-filled, we live into the Sun sphere. As we proceed we enter into a realm where the Sun is now below us, as previously was the earth. We look back towards the Sun, and this is the beginning of something strange. We become aware that we have to recognize yet another being, the spirit of Lucifer.

The nature of Lucifer cannot be rightly evaluated after death unless we have previously done so by means of spiritual science or initiation. It is only when we arrive beyond the Sun sphere that we recognize him as he was before he became Lucifer, when he was still a brother of Christ. Lucifer changed only in the course of time because he remained behind and severed himself from the stream of cosmic progress. His harmful influence does not extend beyond the Sun sphere. Above this there is still another sphere where Lucifer can unfold his activity as it was before the severance. He does not unfold anything harmful there, and if we have united ourselves rightly with the Mystery of Golgotha, we journey onward led by Christ and are rightly received by Lucifer into yet further spheres of the universe. The name Lucifer was correctly chosen, as indeed names were wisely given in olden times. The Sun is below us and so is the light of the Sun. Now we need a new light-bearer who illumines our path into the universe.

Thus, we arrive in the Mars sphere. As long as we dwelt below the Sun, we gazed towards the Sun. The Sun is now below us and we look out into the widths of universal space. We experience the widths of universal space through what is often referred to but little understood as the harmony of the spheres, a kind of spiritual music. The visions in which we are enveloped hold less and less significance for us. Increasingly what we hear spiritually grows meaningful. The heavenly bodies do not appear as they do in earthly astronomy that measures their relative speeds. In fact, the faster or slower sounding together produces the tones of the music of the spheres. Inwardly the human being feels increasingly that only what he has received of the spirit on earth remains for him in this sphere. This enables him to make the acquaintance of the beings of this sphere and retain his sociability. People who cut themselves off from the spiritual nowadays cannot enter the spiritual world in spite of their moral inclination and religious disposition. Nothing can be done about it, although it is of course possible that such people draw near to the spirit in the next incarnation.

Without exception all materialistically inclined people become hermits once they have gone beyond the Sun into the Mars sphere. It may sound foolish, yet it is true that the Monistic Union will not survive once its adherents have reached the Sun sphere because, as each of them is a hermit, they cannot possibly meet.

A person who has acquired spiritual understanding on earth will have yet another experience on Mars. As we are speaking more intimately today, I shall relate it. The question can be put within our own world conception that we develop as spiritual science in the western world. What has happened to Buddha since his last earthly incarnation? I have mentioned this on previous occasions. Buddha lived as Gautama during his last incarnation six hundred years B.C. If you have studied my lectures carefully you will recall that he has worked since on another occasion when he did not incarnate as Buddha, but only worked spiritually at the birth of the Luke Jesus-child. Spiritually he sent his influence from higher spheres unto the earth. But where is he? In Sweden at Norrköping I drew attention to yet a later influence of the Buddha on the earth. During the eighth century at a Mystery Center in Europe on the Black

Sea, Buddha lived spiritually in one of his disciples. This disciple was later to become Francis of Assisi. So Francis of Assisi was in his previous incarnation a pupil of Buddha and absorbed all the qualities necessary for him to work later in the extraordinary way he did. In many respects his followers cannot be distinguished from those of Buddha, except that the ones were disciples of Buddha and the others were Christians. This was due to the fact that in his previous incarnation he was a pupil of Buddha, of the spiritual Buddha. But where is the actual Buddha, the one who lived as Gautama? He became for Mars what Christ has become for the earth. He accomplished a kind of Mystery of Golgotha for Mars and brought about the extraordinary redemption of the Mars inhabitants. He dwells there among them. His earthly life was the right preparation in order to redeem the Mars inhabitants, but his redeeming deed was not quite like the Mystery of Golgotha. It was somewhat different.

Spiritually, man lives in the Mars sphere as indicated. Then he proceeds further and lives into the Jupiter sphere. His connection with the earth, which up until now still continued slightly, has become quite meaningless. The Sun still has a limited influence on him, but now the Cosmos begins to work powerfully upon him. Everything is now working from outside, and man receives cosmic influences. The entire Cosmos works through the harmony of the spheres, which assumes even other forms the further we investigate life between death and rebirth. It is not easy to characterize the change that occurs in the harmony of the spheres. As it cannot be expressed in words, we may use an analogy. The harmony of the spheres transforms itself in the passage from Mars to Jupiter as orchestral music would change into choral music. Jupiter as orchestral music would change into choral music. It becomes increasingly tone, filled with meaning, expressive of its actual being. The harmony of the spheres receives content as we ascend into the sphere of Jupiter, and in the Saturn sphere full content is bestowed upon it as the expression of the Cosmic Word out of which everything has been created and which is found in the Gospel of St. John, "In the beginning was the Word." In this Word cosmic order and cosmic wisdom sound forth.

Now the one who is prepared proceeds into other spheres —the spiritual person farther, the less spiritual not so far —but he comes into quite a different condition from the previous one. One might characterize it thus. Beyond Saturn a spiritual sleep begins, whereas during the previous stages one was spiritually awake. From now onward consciousness is dimmed, man dwells in a benumbed condition that makes it possible for him to undergo still other experiences. Just as in sleep we do away with tiredness and gather new forces, so as a result of the dimming of consciousness, when we have become a fully expanded spatial sphere, spiritual forces stream in from the cosmos. First we have sensed it, then we have heard it as a universal orchestra. Then it has sung forth and we have perceived it as the Word. Then we fall asleep and it penetrates us. During this period we again travel through all the spheres, but with a dimmed consciousness. Our consciousness becomes ever dimmer. We now contract, quickly or slowly according to our karma, and during this process of contraction we come once more under the influence of the forces emanating from the Sun system. We journey back from sphere to sphere through the cosmos. Now we are not sensitive to influence from the Moon sphere. We proceed, unaffected, unhampered, as it were, and continue to contract until we unite ourselves with the small human germ that goes through its development before birth.

Unless physiology and embryology receive their facts from occult investigation, they cannot contain the truth, for the embryo is a reflection of the vast cosmos. The whole cosmos is carried within it. The human being carries as a potential power within him what happens physically between conception and birth, and also what he undergoes during the period of cosmic sleep.

Here we touch upon a wonderful mystery. It actually only has been indicated or portrayed in our time by artists. In the future it will be understood better. We shall come to experience what really lives in the Tristan story, in the Tristan mood. We shall understand that the whole cosmos streams into the love of Tristan and Isolde, and we shall recognize it truly as the course of man's development between death and rebirth. What has been gathered from the cosmos, from Saturn, influences lovers who are brought together. Many things are turned into cosmic events. They should not be analyzed intellectually, but we should experience what connects man truly to the whole cosmos. That is why spiritual science will certainly succeed in developing a new sense of devotion, a true religion in people, because it will be understood that often the smallest things have their origin in the cosmos. We learn rightly and wisely to relate what lives in the human breast to its origin when we consider its connection with the cosmos. Thus, from spiritual science an impulse can pour out for the whole of life, for the whole of mankind, towards a really new attitude that has to come. Artists have prepared it, but a true understanding must be created first through a spiritual inclination.

I wanted to convey these indications on the basis of renewed, intimate investigations of the life of man between death and rebirth. There is nothing in spiritual science that will not also move us in our deepest feelings. When rightly understood nothing remains a mere abstract representation. The flower we behold gives more joy to us than when the botanist tears it to shreds. The far distant starry world can evoke a vague sensing in us, but the reality only dawns when we are able to ascend into the heavenly spheres with our soul. We rob the plant by our dissection, but not the starry world when we ascend beyond the plant and recognize how the spirit is related to it.

Kant made the remarkable utterance of a man who understands morality in a one-sided way. Two things moved him deeply—the starry heavens above and the moral law within. Both are really the same. We only gather them into us out of heavenly realms. If we are born with a moral inclination, it means that on the return journey during the condition of sleep the Mercury sphere was able to bestow much upon us. It was the Venus sphere, if we are endowed with religious feelings. As every morning on earth we awaken strengthened and refreshed with new forces, so we are born strengthened by the forces given by the cosmos, and we receive them in accordance with our karma. The cosmos can bestow forces that are predispositions from birth, inasmuch as karma will allow.

Life between death and rebirth falls into two parts. To begin with it is unalterable. We ascend, the beings approach us. We enter into a condition of sleep and then change can occur. The forces now enter with which we are born. Considering the evolution of man in this way, we see that the human being after death first lives in a world of visions. He only learns to recognize later what he really is as a soul-spiritual being. Beings approach us from outside and they illumine us as the golden light of the morning illuminates the things of the outer world. Thus we ascend and the spiritual world penetrates into us. We do not live into the spiritual world from outside until we have become mature enough to experience what we are in our visionary world, until we encounter the beings of the spiritual world who approach us from all sides like rays.

Transfer yourself into the spiritual world as if you could behold it. There a man emerges, in the form of a visionary cloud, as he truly is. Then the beings can approach and illumine him from outside. We cannot see the rose when it is dark. We switch on the light and because the light falls on the rose we can see it as it really is. So it is when the human being ascends into the spiritual world. The light of the spiritual beings draws near to him. But there is one moment when he is clearly visible, illumined by the light of the Hierarchies so that he reflects back the whole of the outer world. The entire cosmos now appears as if reflected by man. You can imagine the process. First you live on as a cloud that is not sufficiently illumined, then you ray back the light of the cosmos and then you dissolve. There is a moment when man reflects back the cosmic light. Up to this point he can ascend. Dante says in his *Divine Comedy* that in a particular part of the spiritual world one beholds God as man. This is to be taken literally, otherwise it would not make any sense at all. One can of course accept it as a beautiful thought, as aesthetes do, and fail to understand its inner content. This is again an instance where we find the spiritual world mirrored in the works of great artists and poets. This is also the case with the great musicians of more recent times, in a Beethoven, a Wagner and Bruckner. It can happen with one as it did with me a few days ago, when I had to resist a certain piece of knowledge because it was too astonishing.

In Florence we find the Medici Chapel where Michelangelo created two memorial statues to the Medici and four allegorical figures representing "Day" and "Night," "Dawn" and "Dusk." One easily speaks about a cold allegory, but when one looks at these four figures they appear anything but a cold allegory. One of the figures represents "Night." Actually, research in this domain is not particularly enlightened, for you will find it mentioned everywhere that of the two Medici statues depicting Lorenzo and Giuliano, Lorenzo is the thinker. But occult investigation has confirmed that the opposite is true. The one said to be Lorenzo by art historians is Giuliano, and vice versa.

This can be proved historically with reference to the natures of the two personalities. The statues rest on pedestals, and it is likely that in the course of time they have been interchanged. But this is not really what I wanted to say. I only draw your attention to this to show that in this respect outer research misses the mark!

The figure "Night" can be made the object of a fine artistic study. The gesture, the position of the resting body with the head supported by the hand, the arm placed on the leg—in fact the whole arrangement of the figure can be studied artistically. We can sum it up by saying that if one wished to portray the human etheric body in its full activity, then one could only represent it in the form of this figure. That is the outer gesture expressing a human being at rest. When man sleeps, the etheric body is most active. In the figure of "Night" Michelangelo has created the corresponding position. This reclining figure represents the most expressive portrayal of the active etheric or life body.

Now let us go over to "Day" which lies on the opposite side. This represents the most perfect expression of the ego; the figure "Dawn," of the astral body; "Twilight," of the physical body. These are not allegories, but truths taken from life, immortalized with remarkable artistic penetration. I kept away from this knowledge, but the more accurately I studied it, the clearer it became. I am no longer astonished at the legend that originated in Florence at the time. It tells that Michelangelo had power over "Night" and when he was alone with her in the Chapel she would stand up and walk about. As she represents the etheric body, it is not surprising. I only mention this in order to show how clear and intelligible everything becomes the more we view it from the aspect of occultism.

The greatest contribution to the development of spiritual life and culture will be accomplished when human beings meet in such a way that each presupposes and then senses the occultly hidden in the other. Then will the right relationship be established from man to man, and love will permeate the soul in a truly human way. Man will meet man in such a way that one will sense the sacred mystery of the other. It is only in such a relationship that the right feelings of love can be cultivated.

Spiritual science will not have to stress continually the outer cultivation of general human love, but it will receive by way of genuine knowledge the power of love in the soul of man.

LIFE BETWEEN DEATH AND REBIRTH

Munich, November 26–28, 1912

V

LIFE BETWEEN DEATH AND REBIRTH

Munich, November 26, 1912

IT HAS often been explained that it is not as easy to investigate and describe the realm of the occult as is commonly thought. If one wishes to proceed conscientiously in this domain, one will feel it necessary to make repeatedly fresh investigations into important chapters of spiritual research. In recent months it has been my task, among many other things, to make new investigations into a subject of which we have often spoken here. New aspects emerge as a result of such investigations.

Today we shall deal again with the life between death and rebirth, although it can only be done in outline. This does not mean that what has previously been said has to be changed in any way. Precisely in connection with this chapter this is not the case, but in the study of supersensible facts we should always consider them from as many points of view as possible. So today we will consider from a universal standpoint much of what has been presented in my books *Theosophy* or *Occult Science* more from the aspect of immediate human experience. The facts are the same, but we should not imagine that we are fully conversant with them when they have been described from one point of view only. Occult facts are such that we must move around them, so to speak, and examine them from every point of view. In regard to spiritual science the mistake is all too common that judgments are passed by people who may have heard a few statements about a subject without having had the patience to allow what can be said from other aspects to work upon them. Yet the truths of spiritual research can be understood by sound common sense, as was pointed out in yesterday's public lecture.

Today we shall not pay so much attention to the stage after death where the life in kamaloca begins, but rather consider the point at the end of kamaloca when life in the spiritual proper begins. This period lasts until the soul descends into a new incarnation and re-enters earthly life.

Something can be communicated about these matters because, as you know, clairvoyant vision brings one into the same realm in which a human being dwells between death and rebirth. In initiation one experiences, although in a different way, what takes place between death and rebirth. This accounts for the fact that one can communicate something about this realm.

To begin with, I wish to mention two fundamental points of clairvoyant perception that also will help in our understanding of life after death. Attention has often been drawn to the great difference between life in the supersensible world and life in the physical, material world. For instance, the process of knowledge is totally different in the supersensible world from what it is on earth. In the physical world objects present themselves to our senses by making impressions of color and light upon our eyes, audible impressions upon our ears and other impressions upon other sense organs. To perceive objects we must move about in the world. To perceive an object at a distance, we must go towards it. Briefly, in the sense world we must move about to perceive things. The opposite holds true for supersensible perceptions. The quieter the soul, the more everything in the way of inner movement is excluded, the less we strive to draw a thing towards us, the longer we are capable of waiting, the more surely will the perception come and the truer will be the experience we gain from it. In the supersensible world we must allow things to approach us. That is an essential point. We must develop inner silence. Then things will come to us.

The second point I wish to make is this. The way in which the supersensible world confronts us depends on what we bring with us from the ordinary sense world. This is important. It may give rise to considerable soul difficulties in the supersensible world. For instance, it may be exceedingly painful to realize in the supersensible world that we loved a person less than we ought to have done, less than he deserved to be loved by us. This fact stands before the spiritual gaze of one who has entered the supersensible world with far greater intensity than could ever be the case in the physical world. In addition, something else may cause great pain to one with clairvoyant consciousness. None of the forces that we are able to draw from the supersensible world can in any way change or improve a relationship of soul in the physical that we recognize as not having been right. It cannot be made good by forces drawn from the spiritual world. This experience is infinitely more painful than anything we may experience in the physical world. It gives rise to a feeling of powerlessness towards the necessity of karma that can be lived out only in the physical world.

These two factors confront the pupil of occult science

83

after only a little progress. They appear immediately in the life between death and rebirth. Suppose that shortly after death we meet a person who died before us. We encounter him, and we feel the total relationship that we had with him here on earth. We are together with the one who died before, at the same time or after us, and we feel that that is how we stood with him in life. That was our relationship to him. But whereas in the physical world when we realize that we have done an injustice to someone in feeling or in deed, we are able to make the necessary adjustment, we are not able to do so, directly, in the life after death. Clear insight into the nature of the relationship is there, but in spite of the full awareness that it ought to be different, we are incapable of changing anything. To begin with, things must remain as they are. The depression caused by many a reproach is due to the fact that one is clearly aware of the way in which a relationship was not right but it must be left as it is. Yet one feels all the time that it ought to be different. This mood of soul should be transposed to the whole of life after death. After death we realize all the more strongly what we did wrongly during our life on earth but we are incapable of changing anything. Things must take their course, regardless. We look back on what we have done and we must experience wholly the consequences of our actions, knowing full well that nothing can be altered.

It is not only with relationships to other human beings, but with the whole of our soul configuration after death, which depends on a number of factors. To begin with, let me portray life after death in the form of Imaginations. If we take the words "Visions" or "Imaginations" in the sense in which I explained them yesterday, no misunderstanding will arise. Man perceives the physical world through his sense organs. After death he lives in a world of visions, but these visions are mirror-images of reality. Just as here in the physical world we do not immediately perceive the inner nature of the rose, but the external redness, so do we not have a direct perception of a departed friend or brother, but encounter a visionary image. We are enveloped in the cloud of our visions, so to speak, but we know quite clearly that we are together with the other being. It is a real relationship, in fact more real than a relationship between one person and another can be on earth.

In the first period after death we perceive a soul through the image. Also after the kamaloca period the visions that surround us, and that we experience, point back, for the most part, to what we experienced on earth. We know, for instance, that a dead friend is there outside us in the spiritual world. We perceive him through our visions. We feel entirely at one with him. We know exactly how we are related to him. What we chiefly perceive, however, is what happened between us on earth. This, to begin with, clothes itself in our vision. The chief thing is the aftermath of our earthly relationship, just as even after the kamaloca period we live in the consequences of our earthly existence. The cloud of visions that envelops us is entirely dependent on how we spent our earthly existence.

In the first period of kamaloca the soul is clothed, as in a cloud, by its Imaginations. At first the cloud is dark. When some time has elapsed after death, Imaginative vision gradually perceives that this cloud begins to light up as if irradiated by the rays of the morning sun. When Inspiration is added to Imaginative cognition we realize that we live, to begin with, in the cloud of our earthly experiences. We are enveloped by them. We are able to relate ourselves only to those who have died and with whom we were together on the earth, or to those still on earth capable of ascending with their consciousness into the spiritual world. What we have characterized for Imaginative cognition as the illumination of the cloud of our visions from one side by a glimmering light points to the approach of the hierarchies into our own being. We now begin to live into the realm of higher spirituality. Previously, we were only connected to the world we brought with us. Now the life of the higher hierarchies begin to shine towards us, to penetrate us. But in order to understand this process, we must gain some insight into the relationships of size perceived through imaginative cognition as the soul draws out of the physical body.

This actually happens as we pass through the gate of death. Our being expands and becomes larger and larger. This is not an easy concept but that is what actually happens. It is only on earth that we consider ourselves limited within the boundary of our skin. After death we expand into the infinite spaces, growing ever larger. When we have reached the end of the kamaloca period, we literally extend to the orbit of the moon around the earth. In the language of occultism we become Moon dwellers. Our being has expanded to such an extent that its outer boundary coincides with the circle described by the moon around the earth. Today I cannot go into the relative positions of the planets. An explanation of what does not apparently agree with orthodox astronomy can be found in the Düsseldorf lectures, *Spiritual Hierarchies and Their Reflection in the Physical World: Zodiac, Planets, Cosmos.*

Thus we grow farther out into cosmic space, into the

whole planetary system, though first into what the occultist calls the Mercury sphere. That is to say, after the kamaloca period we become Mercury dwellers. We truly feel that we are inhabiting cosmic space. Just as during our physical existence we feel ourselves to be earth dwellers, so then we feel ourselves to be Mercury dwellers. I cannot describe the details now, but the following conscious experience is present. We are not now enclosed in such a small fraction of space as during our earthly existence but the wide sphere bounded by the orbit of Mercury is within our being. How we live through this period also depends upon how we have prepared ourselves on earth—on the forces we have imbibed on earth in order to grow into the right or wrong relationship to the Mercury sphere.

In order to understand these facts we can compare two or more people by means of occult research but we will take two. For instance, let us consider a man who passed through the gate of death with an immoral attitude and one who passed through the gate of death with a moral attitude of soul. A considerable difference is perceptible and it becomes apparent when we consider the relationship of one person to another after death. For the man with a moral attitude of soul, the pictures are present, enveloping the soul and he can have a certain degree of communion everywhere with other human beings. This is due to his moral attitude. A man with an immoral attitude of soul becomes a kind of hermit in the spiritual world. For example, he knows that another human being is also in the spiritual world. He knows that he is together with him but he is unable to emerge from the prison of his cloud of Imaginations and approach him. Morality makes us into social beings in the spiritual world, into beings who can have contact with others. Lack of morality makes us into hermits in the spiritual world and transports us into solitude. This is an important causal connection between what lives in our souls here on earth and what occurs between death and rebirth.

This is true also of the further course of events. At a later period, after having passed through the Mercury sphere, which in the occult we call the Venus sphere, we feel ourselves as Venus dwellers. There between Mercury and Venus, where our cloud of visions is irradiated from without, the Beings of the higher hierarchies are able to approach the human being. Now again it depends on whether we have prepared ourselves in the right manner to be received as social spirits into the ranks of the hierarchies and to have communion with them, or whether we are compelled to pass them by as hermits. Whether we are social or lonely spirits depends upon still another factor. Whereas in the previous sphere we can be sociable only if this has been prepared on earth as a result of morality, in the Venus sphere the power that leads us into community, into a kind of social life, is due to our religious attitude on earth. We most certainly condemn ourselves to become hermits in the Venus sphere if we have failed to develop religious feelings during earthly life, feelings of union with the Infinite, with the Divine. Occult investigation observes that as a result of an atheistic tendency in the soul, of rejecting the connection of our finite with our infinite nature, the human being locks himself up within his own prison. It is a fact that the adherents of the Monistic Union, with its creed that does not promote a truly religious attitude, are preparing themselves for a condition in which they will no longer be able to form any Monistic Union, but will be relegated each to his own separate prison!

This is not meant to be a principle on which to base judgments. It is a fact that presents itself to occult observation as the consequence of a religious or irreligious attitude of soul during earthly life. Many different religions have been established on the earth in the course of evolution, all of them emanating essentially from a common source. Their founders have had to reckon with the temperament of the different peoples, with the climate and with other factors to which the religions had to be adjusted. It is therefore in the nature of things that souls did not come into this Venus sphere with a common religious consciousness, but with one born of their particular creed.

Definite feelings for the spiritual that are colored by this or that religious creed bring it about that in the Venus sphere a man has community only with those of like feelings who shared the same creed during earthly life. In the Venus sphere individuals are separated according to their particular creeds. On the earth they have hitherto been divided into races according to external characteristics. Although the configuration of groups in the Venus sphere corresponds in general to the groupings of people here on earth because racial connections are related to religious creeds, the groupings do not quite correspond because there they are brought together according to their understanding of a particular creed. As a result of experience connected with a particular creed, souls enclose themselves within certain boundaries. In the Mercury sphere a man has, above all, understanding for those with whom he was connected on earth. If he had a moral attitude of soul, he will have real intercourse in the Mercury sphere with those to whom he was related during his earthly life. In the Venus sphere he is taken up into one of the great religious communities to which he belonged during his earthly existence by virtue of his constitution of soul.

The next sphere is the Sun sphere in which we feel ourselves as Sun dwellers for a definite period between death and rebirth. During this period we learn to know the nature of the Sun, which is quite other than astronomy describes. Here again it is a question of living rightly into the Sun sphere. We now have the outstanding experience, and it arises in the soul like an elemental power, that all differentiations between human souls must cease. In the Mercury sphere we are more or less limited to the circle of those with whom we were related on earth. In the Venus sphere we feel at home with those who had similar religious experiences to ours on earth and we still find satisfaction only among these communities. But the soul is conscious of deep loneliness in the Sun sphere if it has no understanding for the souls entering this sphere, as is the case with Felix Balde, for instance. Now in ancient times conditions were such that in the Venus sphere souls were to be found in the provinces of the several religions, finding and giving understanding in them. Because all religions have sprung from a common source, when the human being entered the Sun sphere he had in him so much of the old common inheritance that he could come near to all the other souls in the Sun sphere and be together with them, to understand them, to be a social spirit among them.

In these more ancient periods of evolution souls could not do much of themselves to satisfy the longing that arose there. Because without human intervention a common human nucleus was present in mankind, it was possible for souls to have intercourse with others belonging to different creeds. In ancient Brahmanism, in the Chinese and other religions of the earth, there was so much of the common kernel of religion that souls in the Sun sphere found themselves in that primal home, the source of all religious life. This changed in the middle period of the earth. Connection with the primal source of the religions was lost and can only be found again through occult knowledge. So, in the present cycle of evolution man also must prepare himself for entering the Sun sphere while still on earth because community does not arise there of itself. This is also an aspect of the significance of the Mystery of Golgotha, of Christianity. Because of it human beings in the present cycle of evolution can so prepare themselves on earth that universal community is achieved in the Sun sphere. For this purpose the Sun Spirit, the Christ, had to come down to earth. Since His coming, it has been possible for souls on the earth to find the way to universal community in the Sun sphere between death and rebirth.

Much could be added in support of the universality that is born of the Christ Mystery when it is rightly understood. Much has been said in the course of years, but the Christ Mystery can ever and again be illuminated from new aspects. It is often said that special emphasis of the Christ Mystery creates prejudices against other creeds, and that is advanced because in our Anthroposophical Movement in Central Europe special emphasis has been laid on it. Such a reproach is quite unintelligible. The true meaning of the Christ Mystery has only been discovered from the occult aspect in modern times. If a Buddhist were to say, "You place Christianity above Buddhism because you attribute a special position to the Christ that is not indicated in my sacred books, and you are therefore prejudiced against Buddhism," that would be as sensible as if the Buddhist were to claim that the Copernican view of the universe cannot be accepted because it, too, is not contained in his sacred writings. The fact that things are discovered at a later date has nothing to do with the equal justification of religious beliefs.

The Mystery of Golgotha is such that it cannot be regarded as a special privilege. It is a spiritual-scientific fact that can be acknowledged by every religious system just as the Copernican system can. It is not a question of justifying some creed that up until now has failed to understand the Mystery of Golgotha, but rather is it a question of grasping the spiritual-scientific fact of Golgotha. If this is unintelligible, it is even more so to speak about an abstract comparison of all creeds and to say that one ought to accept an abstract similarity among them. The different creeds should not be compared with what Christianity has become as a creed, but with the essence that is contained in Christianity itself.

Take the Hindu creed. Nobody is received into this creed who is not a Hindu. It is connected with a people, and this is true of most ancient creeds. Buddhism has broken through this restriction, yet if rightly understood, it too applies to a particular community. But now let us consider the external facts. If in Europe we were to have a creed similar, let us say, to the Hindu creed, we should be obliged to swear allegiance to the ancient god, Wotan. Wotan was a national god, a god connected with a definite racial stock. But what has in fact happened in the West? It is not a national god that has been accepted, but, inasmuch as his external life is concerned, an alien personality. Jesus of Nazareth has been accepted from outside. Whereas the other creeds essentially have something egoistical about them in the religious sense and do not wish to break through their boundaries, the West has been singled out by the fact that it has suppressed its egoistical religious system—for example, the ancient Wotan religion—and for the sake of its inner substance has accepted an impulse that did not grow out of its own flesh and blood. Insofar as the West is concerned, Christianity is not the egoistical creed that the others were for the different peoples. This is a factor of considerable importance that is also borne out by external happenings. It makes for the universality of Christianity in yet another respect if Christianity truly places the Mystery of Golgotha at the center of the evolution of humanity.

Christianity has not yet made great progress in its development because even now two aspects have still not been clearly distinguished. They will only be distinguished slowly and by degrees. Who, in the true sense of the Mystery of Golgotha, is a Christian? He is one who knows that something real happened in the Mystery of Golgotha, that the Sun Spirit lived in the Christ, that Christ poured His Being over the earth, that Christ died for all men. Although Paul declared that Christ died not only for the Jews but also for the heathen, these words even today are still little understood. Not until it is realized that Christ fulfilled the Deed of Golgotha for all human beings will Christianity be understood. For the real power that flowed from Golgotha is one thing, and the understanding of it is another. Knowledge of who the Christ really is should be striven for, but since the Mystery of Golgotha our attitude to every man can only be expressed as follows. Whatever your creed may be, Christ also died for you, and His significance for you is the same as for every other human being.

A true understanding of the Mystery of Golgotha leads to the attitude that we ask ourselves about each person we meet, "How much has he in him of real Christianity, irrespective of his particular belief?" Because man must increasingly acquire consciousness of what is real in him, to know something of the Mystery of Christ is naturally a lofty ideal. This will become more widespread as time goes on, and to it will belong the need to understand the Mystery of Golgotha. But this is different from the concept that one may have of the Mystery of Golgotha, of its universality that holds good for all human beings. Here the essential thing is for the soul to feel that this makes us into social beings in the Sun sphere. If we feel enclosed in some creed, we become hermits there. We are social beings in the Sun sphere if we understand the universality of the Mystery of Golgotha. Then we can find a relation to every being who draws near to us in the Sun sphere. As a result of the insight into the Mystery of Golgotha that we acquire during earthly life within our cycle of evolution, we become beings able to move freely in the Sun sphere.

Of what should we be capable during this period between death and rebirth?

We come now to a fact that is exceedingly important for modern occultism. Those human beings who lived on earth before the Mystery of Golgotha—what I am now saying is essentially correct, though not in detail—found the Throne of Christ in the Sun sphere with the Christ upon it. They were able to recognize Him because the old legacy of the common source of all religions was still living in them. But the Christ Spirit came down from the Sun, and in the Mystery of Golgotha He flowed into the life of the earth. He left the Sun, and only the Akashic picture of the Christ is found in the Sun sphere between death and rebirth. The Throne is not occupied by the real Christ. We must bring up from the earth the concept of our living connection with Christ in order that through the Akashic picture we have a living relationship with Him. Then it is possible for us to have the Christ also from the Sun sphere and for Him to stimulate all the forces in us that are necessary if we are to pass through the Sun sphere in the right way.

Our journey between death and rebirth progresses still further. From the earthly realm we have derived the power, through a moral and religious attitude of soul, to live, as it were, into the human beings with whom we were together on the earth, and then into the higher hierarchies. But this power gradually vanishes, becomes dimmer and dimmer, and what remains is essentially the power that we derive on the earth from the Mystery of Golgotha. In order that we may find our way in the Sun sphere a new Light-bearer appears there, a Being whom we must learn to know in his primal power. We bring with us from the earth an understanding of the Christ, but in order to develop a stage further so that we may proceed out into the universe from the Sun sphere to Mars, we need to recognize the second Throne that stands beside the Throne of Christ in the Sun. This is possible simply by virtue of the fact that we are human souls. From this other Throne we now learn to know the other Being who, together with the Christ, leads us onward. This other Being is Lucifer. We learn to know Lucifer, and through the powers that he is able to impart to us

95

we make the further journey through the spheres of Mars, Jupiter and Saturn.

We expand ever further into cosmic space, but as we move out beyond the Saturn sphere our state of consciousness is changed. We enter into a kind of cosmic twilight. We cannot call it a cosmic sleep, but a cosmic twilight. Now for the first time the powers of the whole cosmos can work in upon us. They work from all sides, and we receive them into our being. So after we have expanded into these spheres, there is a period between death and rebirth when the forces of the whole cosmos stream into our being from all sides, from the whole of the starry realms, as it were. Then we begin to draw together again, pass through the different spheres down to the Venus sphere, contract and become ever smaller until the time comes when we can again unite with an earthly human germ.

What kind of a being are we when we unite with this germ? We are the being we have described, but we have received into us the forces from the whole cosmos. What we receive during the outward journey depends on the extent to which we have prepared ourselves for it, and our karma is formed according to the way we have lived together with the human beings we have met during life on earth. The forces by means of which an adjustment takes place in a new earth life are built up as a result of having been together with those human beings after death. That we appear as a human being, that we are inwardly able to have karma imbued with cosmic forces, depends on the fact that we received forces from the whole cosmos during a certain period between death and a new birth. At birth a being who has contracted to the minutest dimensions, but has drawn into itself the forces of the wide expanse of the whole cosmos unites itself with the physical human germ. We bear the whole cosmos within us when we incarnate again on earth. It may be said that we bear this cosmos within us in the way in which it can unite with the attitude that we, in accordance with our earlier earth existence, had brought with us in our souls on the outward journey when we were expanding into the spheres.

A twofold adaptation has to take place. We adapt to the whole cosmos and to our former karma. The fact that there is also an adaptation to former karma that must be harmonized in the cosmos came to me in an extraordinary way during the investigations of the last few months in connection with individual cases. I say, expressly, in individual cases because I do not wish to state thereby a general law. When a person passes through the gate of death he dies under a certain constellation of stars. This constellation is significant for his further life of soul because it remains there as an imprint. In his soul there remains the endeavor to enter into this same constellation at a new birth, to do justice once again to the forces received at the moment of death. It is an interesting point that if one works out the constellation at death and compares it with the constellation of the later birth, one finds that it coincides to a high degree with the constellation at the former death. It must be remembered that the person is born at another spot on the earth that corresponds with this constellation. In fact, he is adapted to the cosmos, members himself into the cosmos, and thus a balance is established in the soul between the individual and the cosmic life.

Kant once said very beautifully that there were two things that especially uplifted him—the starry heavens above him and the moral law within him. This is a beautiful expression in that it is confirmed by occultism. Both are the same—the starry heavens above us and what we bear as moral law within us. For as we grow out into cosmic space between death and a new birth, we take the starry heavens into ourselves, and then in the soul we bear as our moral attitude a mirror image of the starry heavens. Here we touch upon one of the points where anthroposophy can only develop into a feeling for the moral-universal. What appears to be theory is immediately transformed into moral impulses of the soul. Here the human being feels full responsibility towards his own being, for he realizes that between death and a new birth the whole cosmos worked into his being, and he gathered together what he derived from the cosmos. He is responsible to the whole cosmos, for he actually bears the whole of the cosmos within him.

An attempt has been made to express this feeling in a passage of *The Soul's Probation*, in the monologue of Capesius, where it is said, "In your thinking world-thoughts are weaving . . ." Attention is drawn to the significance for the soul when it feels that it is man's sacred duty to bring forth the forces that one has gathered out of the cosmos, and it is the greatest sin to allow these forces to lie fallow.

Concrete investigations showed that we take the whole cosmos into our being and bring it forth again in our earthly existence. Of the forces that man carries with him, only a few have their origin on the earth. We study man in connection with the forces that work in the physical, etheric and astral bodies, and in the ego. Of course, the forces that play into our physical body come to us from the earth, but we cannot draw directly out of the earth the forces we need for the etheric body. These forces can only approach us between death and rebirth during the period we are expanding into the planetary spheres. If one takes an immoral attitude of soul into these spheres, one will not be able to attract the right forces during the time between death and a new rebirth. A man who has not developed religious impulses cannot attract the right forces in the Venus sphere, and so the forces that are needed in the etheric may be stultified. Here we see the karmic connection that exists between later and earlier lives. This indicates how the knowledge that we obtain through occultism may become impulses in our life of soul and how the awareness of what we are can lead us to rise to an ever more spiritual life.

What was prepared for by the Mystery of Golgotha is necessary in our present cycle of evolution so that man may live in the right way into the Sun sphere between death and a new birth. Spiritual science has to achieve that the human being shall be in a position to grow out even beyond the Sun sphere with the universal-human, spiritually social consciousness that is needed there. Insofar as the Sun sphere itself is concerned, the connection that is experienced with the Mystery of Golgotha suffices. But in order to carry a feeling and understanding of the human-universal beyond the Sun sphere, we must be able to grasp, in the anthroposophical sense, the relation of the several religions to one another. We must grow beyond a narrowly circumscribed creed with its particular shades of feeling and understand every soul, irrespective of its belief. Above all, one thing connected with the Christ impulse is fulfilled between death and rebirth. It is contained in the words, "Where two or three are gathered together in my Name, there am I in the midst of them." The gathering of two or three is not connected by Christ with this or that belief.

The possibility of Him being among them is provided inasmuch as they are united in His Name.

What has been cultivated for years, through the performances of the Mystery Plays, and especially the last (*The Guardian of the Threshold*), should provide a spiritual-scientific understanding for what is essential in our epoch. On the one hand, we have to acquire a relationship to the Christ impulse, on the other, to the Powers that stand in opposition to Him—the impulses of Lucifer and Ahriman. We must realize that as soon as we emerge from Maya, we have to deal with Powers who unfold forces in the cosmos. The time is drawing ever nearer in the evolution of humanity when we must learn to discern the essential being rather than the teaching. This is nowhere so apparent as in connection with the Mystery of Golgotha. The Being is essential, not the mere content of the words.

I should like the following to be put quite exactly to the test. In fact, it is easiest to deal with people who put to the test what is said out of occult sources. There is nothing similar in any of the other creeds to the depths that are revealed through the Mystery of Golgotha.

A particular prejudice still prevails today. People speak as if things should happen in the world as they do in a school, as if everything depended on the World Teacher. But the Christ is not a World Teacher but a World Doer, One Who has fulfilled the Mystery of Golgotha, and Whose Being should be recognized. That is the point. How little it is a question of the mere words, of the mere doctrinal content, we learn from the beautiful words uttered by the Christ, "Ye are Gods!" (John 10, 34). We learn this also from the fact that He indicated repeatedly that man attains the highest when he realizes the divine in his own nature.

These words of the Christ resound into the world, "Be conscious that you are like the Gods!" One can say that that is a great teaching!

The same teaching, however, resounds from other sources. In the Bible, where the beginning of Earth evolution is described, Lucifer says, "Ye shall be as Gods!" The same doctrinal content is uttered by Lucifer and by the Christ, "Ye shall be as Gods!" but the two utterances mean the opposite for man. Indeed, shattering calls sound forth in these words uttered at one time by the Tempter and at another by Him Who is the Redeemer, the Savior and the Restorer of the being of man.

Between death and rebirth everything depends upon knowledge of the *Being*. In the Sun sphere the greatest danger is to take Lucifer for the Christ because both use the same language, as it were, give the same teaching, and from them both the same words resound forth. Everything depends on the *Being*. The fact that this Being or that Being is speaking—that is the point, not the doctrinal content because it is the real forces pulsing through the world that matter. In the higher worlds, and above all in what plays into the earthly spheres, we only understand the words aright when we know from which Being they proceed. We can never recognize the rank of a Being merely by the word, but only by knowledge of the whole connection in which a Being stands. The example of the words that men are like the Gods is an absolute confirmation of this.

These are significant facts of evolution. They are voiced not on account of their content—and in this case, too, not so much on this account—but on account of the spirit they carry, so that there may arise in souls feelings that ought to be the outcome of such words. If the feelings remain with those who have absorbed such truths, even if the actual words are forgotten, not so much is lost, after all. Let us take the most radical case. Suppose that there were someone among us who would forget everything that had just been said, but would only retain the feeling that can flow from such words. Such a person would, nevertheless, in an anthroposophical sense, receive enough of what is meant by them.

After all, we have to make use of words, and words sometimes appear theoretical. We must learn to look through the words to the essence and receive this into the soul. If anthroposophy is grasped in its essence, the world will learn to understand many things, particularly in connection with the evolution of humanity. Here I want to quote two examples that are connected outwardly, rather than inwardly, with my recent occult investigations. They astonished me because they showed how a truth which was established occultly corresponds to what has come into the world as a result of inspired men and can be rediscovered in what exists already in the world.

I have occupied myself a great deal with Homer. Lately the fact that nothing can be changed after death, that relationships remain the same, came vividly before my soul. For example, if in life one was in some way related to a person and did not love him, this cannot be changed. If, bearing this in mind, one now reads the passages in Homer where he describes the world beyond as a place where life becomes unchangeable, one begins to understand the depth of these words about the region where things are no longer subject to change. It is a wonderful experience to compare one's own knowledge with what was expressed as significant occult truth by the "blind Homer," the seer, in his epic!

Another fact astounded me, and though I strongly resisted it because it seemed incredible, I found it impossible to do so. Many of you will know the Medici Tombs by Michelangelo in Florence, with the statues of Giuliano and Lorenzo de Medici and four allegorical figures. The artistic element in these figures is usually overlooked. They are viewed as barren allegories. Now these figures with one exception, were not quite finished, and yet they do not give the impression of being merely allegorical. In the guide books we are told that the statue of Giuliano stands on one side and that of Lorenzo on the other. Actually, they have been reversed. The statue said to represent Lorenzo is that of Giuliano, and that of Giuliano is the statue of Lorenzo. This is correct, but in almost every history of art manual, and in Baedecker, the facts are wrongly given. The descriptions would certainly not tally and apparently the statues were once reversed. They no longer stand where Michelangelo had placed them originally. But I want to speak mainly about the four allegorical figures. At the foot of one of the Medici statues we have the figures of "Night" and "Day;" at the foot of the other, "Dawn" and "Dusk."

As I said, to begin with I resisted what I am now going to say about them. Let us start with the figure of "Night." Suppose one immerses oneself in everything one sees, in every gesture (books comment rather nonsensically that this is a gesture that a sleeping person cannot possibly adopt). If, having studied every gesture, every movement of the limbs, one asks oneself how an artist would have to portray the human figure if he wished to convey the greatest possible activity of the etheric body in sleep, then he would have to do it out of his artistic instincts exactly as Michelangelo did it in his figure. The figure of "Night" corresponds with the posture of the etheric body. I am not suggesting that Michelangelo was conscious of this. He simply did it.

Now let us look at the figure of "Day." This is no barren allegory. Picture the lower members of the human being more passive, and the ego predominantly active. We have this expressed in the figure of "Day." If we were now to express in the posture the action of the astral body working freely when the other members are reduced to inactivity, then we should find this in the so-called allegory of "Dawn." And if we sought to express the conditions where the physical body is not altogether falling to pieces, but becomes limp as a result of the withdrawal of the ego and astral body, this is wonderfully portrayed in the figure of "Dusk." In these figures we have living portrayals of the four sheaths of man. We can readily understand the once widespread legend about the figure "Night." It was said that when Michelangelo was alone with this figure it became alive, rose up and walked about. This is understandable if one knows that it has the posture of the etheric or life body, and that in such a position the etheric body can be fully active. If this is perceived, then indeed the figure appears to rise up, and one knows that it could walk about were it not carved out of marble. If the etheric body only were really active there, then nothing would prevent it from moving about.

Many secrets are contained in the works of men, and much will become intelligible for the first time when these things are studied with sharpened occult perception.

Whether, however, we understand a work of art well or not so well, is not connected with the universal-human. What matters is something quite else. If our eyes are sharpened in this way we begin to understand the soul of another human being, not through occult perception, which, after all, cannot help seeing into the spiritual world, but through a perception quickened by spiritual science. Spiritual science grasped by sound human reason develops knowledge in us of what we meet in life, and, above all, of the souls of our fellow men. We shall attempt to understand every human soul.

This understanding, however, is meant in quite a different way from the usual. Unfortunately, in life love is all too often entirely egotistical. Usually a man loves what he is particularly attracted to because of some circumstance or other. For the rest, he contents himself with universal love, a general love for humanity. But what is this? We should be able to understand every human soul. We will not find excellence everywhere, but no harm is done for actually one can do no greater injury to some souls than by pouring blind love and adulation over them.

We shall speak further on this subject in the lecture the day after tomorrow.

VI

LIFE BETWEEN DEATH AND REBIRTH

Munich, November 28, 1912

THE LECTURE given the day before yesterday on the conditions between death and a new birth shows how closely the whole being of man is connected with the universal life in the cosmos. It is really only during his earthly life that the human being is fixed to one place, occupies a small space, whereas during the period between death and a new birth he is part of the planetary system and, at a later period after death, even of the world beyond the planetary system. In his development between birth and death the human being is the expression of a microcosmic image of the macrocosm, so between death and a new birth he is macrocosmic; he is poured out into the macrocosm. He is a macrocosmic being, and he must draw forth from the macrocosm the forces he needs for his next incarnation.

During the first period after death man still bears the shells of earthly life around him. He is connected with what earthly life gave him and was able to make of him. This period is especially close to the needs and the interests of the heart. Occult vision observes someone who has left the physical plane a comparatively short time ago in the sphere of kamaloca, which extends in the macrocosmic sense to the orbit of the Moon. Man's soul and spirit expand in such

106

a way that he dwells in the whole Moon sphere. During this period he is still entirely bound up with the earthly world. The wishes, desires, interests, sympathies, antipathies he has developed formerly draw him back to the earthly world. During the kamaloca period he is enclosed within the atmosphere of his own astral nature acquired on the earth. He still wishes to have what he wished to have on earth. He is interested in the things that interested him on earth. The reason for this kamaloca period is that he may put away these interests, and inasmuch as they are dependent on physical organs, and this is true of all sense enjoyment, they cannot be satisfied. Gradually he is weaned from them precisely because they cannot be satisfied. It will be understood that this refers to the individuality of man in the narrowest sense, to that part of the astrality of a human being that has to be extirpated, removed.

In yet another respect man bears his earthly connections with him into kamaloca, for the beings or events that he will encounter there are dependent upon the nature of his inner life, the disposition of his soul. For instance, let us consider a man who goes through the gate of death and another to whom he had a close relationship who passed somewhat earlier through the gate of death. Both are in kamaloca and they may find one another. Occult investigation shows that man is not only concerned with his own development—the process of getting rid of his desires and interests, for instance—but soon after death, following a brief embryonic period of sleep, he is reunited with those individuals to whom he was closely connected on earth. Yet, generally speaking, there is little prospect that a man finds all those who are with him in kamaloca. Space and time relationships, and especially those of space, are quite different there. It is not that one does not approach such beings. A man may come close to them but may not notice them because perception there is born out of the closeness of a connection in life. So, shortly after death in the kamaloca period, a man finds himself in the environment of those with whom he was closely related in life, and thus in the beginning hardly any other beings come into consideration. The relationships after death are still in accordance with what we formerly have developed. In kamaloca we are related to others in exactly the same way as we were on earth except that we cannot do what is still possible here, that is, change the relationship. It remains as it was on the earth. Here we can develop hatred for someone we once loved, or love for one whom we once hated. We can endeavor to transform our relationship. This is not possible in kamaloca.

Suppose we come across a person who died before us. At first we feel related to him in a way that corresponds to the last relationship we had with him on earth. Then, as you know, we live backwards in time. If formerly we had a different relationship, this cannot be produced artificially. We must live backwards quietly and reach the corresponding period of time when we can again experience the relationship we formerly had with him. This again cannot be changed. It expresses itself as it did on earth. One can readily imagine that this is an exceedingly painful experience, and this is true in a certain sense. It is just as if one wished to move, but were chained to the ground. One feels spiritually bound to a relationship that was established on earth. One literally feels in a state of coercion. Naturally, if this condition of coercion is sufficiently intense, the relationship will be painful. Now in order to understand this condition rightly and sense it from the heart, we should not merely imagine it to be painful. In many respects it is so but the dead one is not conscious only of the painful aspect. He is definitely aware that this condition is necessary, and that to avoid such pain would merely mean to create future obstacles in one's path.

What happens as a result of this process? Imagine that after death we are experiencing the relationship we had formed with another person in life. Through the fixed gaze of our perception, through the experience of the relation, forces are formed in our soul, at first in their spiritual prototypes. These are needed so that our karma might lead us rightly into the future, so that we may find ourselves together with the other person in a next incarnation in such a way that the karmic adjustment may come about. The forces necessary for this karmic adjustment are welded together technically, as it were.

To begin with, the dead one can hardly bring about any change in his environment, and yet the instinctive longing to do so does arise at times. Unfulfilled wishes acquire great significance for him but mostly those that do not always come to the surface of consciousness in life. In this connection it is exceedingly important to pay attention to the following. In our everyday life on the physical plane we are conscious of our sympathies and make mental representations of them, too, but below this lies the subconsciousness. This does not rise powerfully into our upper consciousness, into the true ego-consciousness. As a result, something incomplete rises into the consciousness of the human being. Indeed, he hardly ever lives himself out fully as a conscious being in life. Our soul life is exceedingly complex. Man is seldom truly himself. It may happen that out of prejudice, indolence or for some other reason, a man in his ordinary consciousness strongly dislikes or even hates something, while in his subconsciousness there is a powerful longing for the very thing he hates in his upper consciousness. Moreover, the soul frequently tries to delude itself about such matters.

Let us take an example. Two people are living together. One of them comes to anthroposophy and is enthusiastic about it, the other does not share this enthusiasm. In fact, the more the former becomes interested in anthroposophy, the more the latter rages against spiritual science and slanders it. Now the following is possible, for human soul life is complicated. The one who slandered anthroposophy would have become an anthroposophist himself at some time if his friend or the person related to him had not become an anthroposophist. The one who is living with him is the hindrance to his becoming an anthroposophist. This certainly can happen. The one who slanders anthroposophy, bringing forward all manner of things against it in his ego-consciousness, may have the most intense longing for it in his subconsciousness or astral consciousness. Indeed, the more he slanders spiritual science the stronger is his wish for it. It may well occur that a man slanders those things in his upper consciousness that appear all the more strongly in his subconsciousness.

Death, however, transforms untruths into truths. Thus one can observe that human beings passing through the gate of death who out of indolence or for similar reasons have slandered spiritual science, and this is applicable to many other things, experience after death a profound longing of which they were unaware during life. So it can be observed that human beings pass through the gate of death who apparently showed no wish for some particular thing, and in whom, nevertheless, after death a most intense desire for it arises. During our trials in the kamaloca period it is therefore immaterial whether our wishes, desires and passions are present in our upper ego-consciousness or whether they dwell in our astral subconsciousness. Both work as burning factors after death, but those wishes and desires we have concealed during life are even more active after death.

It should be borne in mind that by the very nature of the soul everything connected with it will, under all circumstances, make an impression on it. The following has been carefully investigated and it is good if we take an example in connection with anthroposophy. Suppose two people are living together on earth. One of them is a zealous anthroposophist, the other does not wish to hear anything about spiritual science. Now because spiritual science is in his environment, the latter does not remain uninfluenced by it in his astral body. Things of considerable significance and of which we are not aware are constantly happening to our souls. They work in a spiritual way and there are influences that transform our soul life.

So we find hardly anyone who has lived in the environment of an anthroposophist, however obstinate his opposition, who in his subconscious does not show a leaning towards spiritual science. It is precisely among the opponents of anthroposophy that one finds after death a sphere of wishes in which a passionate longing for spiritual science is manifest. This is why a practice that has become customary among us has proved to be so beneficial for the dead, that is, to read to those who during their lives were unwilling to receive much anthroposophy. This proves to be extraordinarily beneficial for the souls concerned. This should be done by vividly picturing the face of the person who has died as he was during the last period of his life on earth. Then one takes a book and quietly goes through it sentence by sentence with one's thoughts directed towards the dead person as if he were sitting in front of one. He will receive this eagerly and gain much from it.

Here we reach a point where anthroposophy enters into life in a practical way. Here materialism and spirituality do not merely confront one another as theories but as actual forces. In fact, by means of spirituality bridges of communication are created between people irrespective of whether they are living or dead. Out of an active spiritual life we can help the dead in this and many other ways of which we shall speak when the opportunity arises.

If we do not stand within the spiritual life, however, the result is not only a lack of knowledge. It also means that we dwell within a limited sphere of existence encompassed only by the physical world. A materialistically minded person at once loses the connection with one who has passed through the gate of death. This shows how very important it is for the one world to work into the other. If, for instance, the dead person, who has an intense longing to learn something of spiritual wisdom, must forego this wish, it will remain a burden to him. At most, it might be possible, although even in kamaloca this is hardly likely, that he would encounter another soul who has died and with whom he has had such a connection on earth that by the mere nature of the relationship he would find some limited satisfaction. In fact, it hardly comes into the picture as compared with the considerable service and the acts of charity that the living can perform for the dead.

Consider the situation of the dead one. He has some intense wish. In the period after death this wish cannot be satisfied because what we bear in our soul is unchangeably rigidified, but from the earth a stream can flow into this otherwise fixed longing. That is actually the only way in which the things that play into our soul can be altered. Therefore, during the first period after death, for the experience of the dead person much depends on the kind of spiritual understanding that is unfolded by the living who were closely related to him.

By acting in accordance with what may be learned through spiritual science, relationships of quite a different kind can be formed in life, relationships that work over from the one world into the other. In this connection there has not yet been much progress, particularly in making anthroposophy into a life force. So much has to be done still in developing anthroposophy so that real powers arise. It is therefore good to make oneself familiar with the truths of spiritual science and then to direct one's whole way of life in accordance with them. If anthroposophy were understood in this deeper sense, it would pulsate like life blood and there would be less discussion and strife in the world about spiritual theories. We should remember that not only our existence on earth but the whole life of mankind is transformed through spiritual science. Once anthroposophy becomes, by way of an understanding of the ideas, more a matter of the heart, men will act and behave in the anthroposophical spirit, to use trivial words. Then such interrelationships will arise more and more often.

We must now broach a matter that is not so easily acceptable, although it can be grasped if one gives thought to it. Man's knowledge on the physical plane is extraordinarily misleading. It is really most deceptive because on the physical plane he knows no more than the facts and connections that he observes. Whereas for the ordinary scientists or the materialistically minded this is the be-all and end-all of what he terms reality, it constitutes the merest trifle of soul life.

Let me give you an apparently paradoxical example. No doubt we remember Schopenhauer's words that truth must blush because it is paradoxical. Man is aware of facts and combines them intellectually. He knows, for example, that it is half past seven. He goes out of his house and crosses the street. At eight o'clock he has arrived somewhere. He knows this by means of sense perception, through intellectual combination, but in most cases he does not realize why he did not leave his house two or three minutes later than intended. Few people will bother to consider such a fact as leaving a few minutes earlier or later. Nevertheless, this may be of significance.

I will take the grotesque example, but examples of this kind in miniature are constantly happening in life, of a man being three minutes late. Had he left his house punctually he would have been run over and killed, and he was not killed because he was three minutes late. It is unlikely that events will happen in this grotesque manner, and yet they are occurring all the time in such a way more or less, but people are not aware of them. The man started out three minutes late, and just as it is true that he would be dead had he left his house punctually at eight o'clock, it is true that he is now alive. His karma saved him from death because he started three minutes late. Now this may appear unimportant, but it is not so. In fact, a person is only indifferent to such an event to the extent that he is unaware of the true reality. If he knew, he would no longer be indifferent.

If you were aware of the fact that had you left punctually you would be dead, then it would not be a matter of indifference to you. It would actually make a deep impression on you and a profound influence would radiate into your soul as a result of this awareness. You need only recall the significance of such an event for our soul life when such an event actually happens. But is this not tantamount to saying we are continuously going through life with firmly closed eyes? This is in fact true.

A man knows what is occurring externally but he is not aware of what would have happened to him had things gone just a little differently. That means that knowledge of the different possibilities is withheld from his soul. The soul lives indifferently, whereas the knowledge of the various possibilities would shatter or uplift our inner consciousness. Man knows the merest trifle about existing connections. He only knows what emerges from the circumstances. As a result, the life of soul is poor, and what would otherwise be expressed fails to be so. One perhaps would not make such a seemingly paradoxical statement if it were not for the fact that one runs one's head up against it in investigating life after death. Among the many things that arise in the soul we must include what has just been described. After death many things appear vividly before the soul of which it had no inkling during life. After death your soul powerfully realizes that at such a moment you were in danger of your life . . . at such and such a time you threw away your happiness . . . here you were lazy, and had you not been so easy-going you might have been able to do some good. A host of things that one has not experienced confronts one after death. What appears ludicrous actually becomes reality after death. A whole world of which one is not aware in life then comes to expression.

Are not the things of which we have been speaking really there? Let us again take the example in which we started out three minutes later than intended, and that we thereby have avoided death. We are unaware of this. To the materialist the fact of not knowing something is regarded as unimportant. An intelligent person does not attach undue importance to the fact that he knows or does not know something because he realizes that things are simply there whether he be aware of them or not. The play and opposition of forces was there and so were we. All the preparatory conditions for our death were present. Forces were working towards one another. They passed one another by, and yet they approached one another. There are many such cases in life. Something is actually there. We do not perceive it, but it is around us nevertheless.

If in our present cycle of evolution people continually acquire an understanding for the spiritual world, things that cannot exist for sense perception but are nevertheless in our environment will work upon us in a definite way. This leads us to an extraordinarily interesting fact. Suppose that events happen as they have been described, and that we avoid death because we left three minutes late. This will make no impression whatsoever on the materialist. But in the man who gradually unfolds an understanding in his heart for such connections there will be a change. Remember that the development of anthroposophy is only just beginning. If he has understood and lived in anthroposophy, not merely acquired an external understanding of it but really lived in it with his heart and mind, then his experience will be different. He may start three minutes late, thereby avoiding death, but at the moment when death would have struck had the circumstances been different, he will sense something within him that will manifest as a feeling for the various possibilities. This will be the result as anthroposophy becomes the life blood of the soul.

What will happen when we gradually unfold such feelings, when human nature directs itself according to spiritual-scientific understanding? Moments in which something might have happened to us lift us for a short time into a kind of temporary mediumistic condition during which we are able to let the spiritual world shine into our consciousness. Such moments may be exceedingly fruitful when a person is to know consciously something of the working of the dead on him. Moments when events that have not happened are experienced in the way described awaken impressions out of the spiritual world. The whole strange realm of a world of subtle sensing will unfold in those who draw near to anthroposophy.

Humanity is evolving, and only an obtuse person would maintain that the human race has always been endowed with the same soul forces. Soul powers change, and although it is true to say that today man is primarily equipped for external perception upon which he works with his thinking, it is equally true that through experiences of the kind that have been described he will evolve into a period when soul-spiritual forces will develop. In this respect, too, we have the prospect of spiritual science becoming a real force intervening creatively in life. Earlier we considered how influences from the physical plane can be exerted on the life after death, and now we have seen where doors or windows can be created so that the experiences of the dead can be perceived here in earthly life. I also wanted to give you an idea of how opportunities arise to establish communication between the two worlds.

Among the many things that can be said about the life between death and rebirth, and we shall get to know them as time goes on, let me just mention this one today. During the life between death and a new birth we find that essentially three forces—of thinking, of feeling and of will or wish—come to expression in the soul. The forces of thinking or of the intellect express themselves in such a way that our consciousness is either clear or vague; the forces of feeling in that we are more or less compassionate or hardhearted, more or less religious or irreligious in our attitude; the forces of volition and wish in that our deeds are more or less egotistical. Thus these three kinds of forces assert themselves. These soul forces each have a different significance for the life after death.

Let us first consider the intellectual forces. How do they assist us after death? They help to render our conscious experience of the period between death and a new birth particularly clear. In fact, the more we endeavor to think clearly and truly during our physical existence, the greater our efforts to acquire a true knowledge of spiritual realities, the brighter and clearer will be our consciousness between death and a new birth. I will speak quite concretely here. A man, for example, who is untrue in his intellectual qualities, who lacks interest in acquiring real knowledge of the conditions obtaining in the spiritual world, will find that, although a consciousness develops, slowly it will become dim. Strange as it may seem, this dimming of consciousness after death causes us to pass through a certain period more rapidly. We pass the more quickly through the spiritual world the more asleep we are. If, therefore, a man is obtuse in his intellect, although he will retain his consciousness for a time, he will not be able to maintain it beyond a certain point. His obtuseness will bring about a twilight condition, and from then onward his life in the spiritual world will pass rapidly and he will return comparatively soon to a physical body.

It is different with the forces of will and wish. They help us to draw forth from the macrocosmic environment between death and rebirth strong or weak forces that are needed for building up our next earthly existence. A man who enters into these macrocosmic conditions with an immoral attitude of soul will not be able to attract the forces essential to a proper building up of the astral and etheric bodies, which will then be stultified. This produces weaklings or the like. Thus it is morality that makes us capable of drawing the forces from the higher worlds that we need for the following incarnation. Intellectuality and morality are closely connected with what the human becomes as a result of his sojourn in the supersensible world between death and rebirth.

The forces of the heart and of feeling, the innermost forces in the human soul, come before us objectively in the corresponding period between death and a new birth. They are outside us. This is significant. One who is capable of love and compassion lives through his life between death and a new birth surrounded by pictures that promote life and happiness corresponding to the measure of his compassion. These come before the soul as his environment. Pictures of hatred appear to the one who has hated.

At a certain stage of the period between death and a new birth we behold as an outer cosmic painting what we are in our innermost being. There is no better painter than these forces, and the firmament after death is filled with what we truly are in heart and mind. We behold this innermost tableau just as here on earth we behold the firmament of the heavens. Thus we have a firmament between death and a new birth, and it remains with us. It is conditioned by whether we have received the Mystery of Golgotha into the innermost depths of our soul in the sense referred to previously as expressed in the words of St. Paul, "Not I but the Christ in me." If we experience the Christ within us, then we have the possibility during our Sun existence to experience in the surrounding Akasha picture-world the Christ in His most wondrous form, in His manifested glory, as the element in which we live and dwell. This thought need not merely have an egotistical significance. It may also be of objective significance because in our further existence this outspread picture is again taken into the soul and is brought down into our next incarnation. As a result, we do not only make ourselves into better human beings, but also into a better force in the evolution of the earth.

So the efforts we make to transform our heart forces are intimately connected with our faculties in the next life, and we see the technique that is at work in transforming our heart forces into a great cosmic panorama, a cosmic firmament between death and a new birth that is then again incorporated into our being, giving us stronger forces than previously. Thus an all-around strengthening process is the result of the fact that we behold in the period between death and a new birth what has been experienced inwardly in life.

We have once again considered matters of considerable importance relating to the conditions of existence between death and a new birth. They are significant because on earth we are in fact nothing else than what life between death and a new birth has made of us. Furthermore, if we ignore them, we shall be less and less able to gain a true knowledge of our own being. If we ignore the conditions of existence between death and a new birth, we shall be incapable of true action and thinking in times to come. These studies are part of wider matters that can be mentioned in relation to the life between death and a new birth. I wished to make a beginning with a content that is to become more and more the substance of spiritual science.

THE WORKING OF KARMA IN LIFE AFTER DEATH

Bern, December 15, 1912

VII

THE WORKING OF KARMA IN LIFE AFTER DEATH

Bern, December 15, 1912

WE ARE celebrating today the fifth anniversary of the Bern Branch. It is also the first occasion on which we have gathered in this room. Let us hope it will offer a worthy frame for our spiritual work and striving in this city. The fact that we are able to hold our more intimate meetings surrounded by such architectural forms as these is of significance for our spiritual endeavors. We know that in a number of different places such rooms are striven for and already exist. In view of the twofold festive nature of this event, it is appropriate to say a few introductory words about the significance of such forms.

In our strivings we repeatedly come to a threefoldness in one or the other direction that may be termed the sacred triad. We discover it expressed in the human soul as thinking, feeling and willing. If we consider thinking we shall find that in our thinking activity we have to direct ourselves according to objective necessities. If we fail to do so, whether in thinking about the things of the physical plane or about spiritual things, we shall commit the error of not reaching the truth. In relation of our will, also, we must orient ourselves according to certain external moral precepts. Here, too, we have to act according to necessities.

In fact, with regard to both our thinking and our willing the necessities of higher realms play into the physical world.

Man feels truly free only in the realm of his feelings. It is quite different from thinking and willing. We feel most at home in the sphere of feeling and sensation when we are compelled neither by thinking nor by willing, but can surrender to what is purely felt. Why is this so? We sense that our thinking is connected with something, is dependent. We likewise feel a dependency in our willing. In our feelings, however, we are completely ourselves and there we live completely within our own soul, as it were. Why is this so? It is because ultimately our feelings are a mirror picture of a power that lies far beyond our consciousness. Thoughts must be considered as images of what they represent. We must so develop our will that it expresses our duties and responsibilities. In the sphere of feeling we can freely experience what speaks to our soul because, occultly considered, feelings are a mirror image of a realm that does not enter our consciousness. It lies beyond our consciousness and is of a divine spiritual nature.

We might say that the gods seek to educate mankind through thinking and willing. Through feeling the gods allow us to participate in their own creative working, though in a mysterious way. In feeling we have something immediately present in our own souls in which the gods themselves delight.

Now by means of forms as they have been created here, our studies can be accompanied by feelings that draw us closer to the spiritual worlds. This intimacy with the spiritual world must be the result of all our considerations. That is why we can attach a certain importance to such surrounding forms and seek to penetrate what they can mean for us. We look in all directions and feel the power of light and color, which for us can become a revelation of what lives in the spiritual world. What we have to say certainly also can be understood in the barren, dreadful halls unfortunately so prevalent everywhere today. But a real warmth of soul can only come about in spiritual studies when we are surrounded by forms such as these. That this can be so after the first five years of our work here in Bern may be looked upon as the good karma that blesses and accompanies our activities. Therefore, we shall devote this occasion that is festive in a twofold way to considering the significance of spiritual science, of a spiritual knowledge, for modern man.

Much that will be considered today has been spoken about previously but we shall discuss it from new aspects. The spiritual worlds can only become fully intelligible if we consider them from the most varied viewpoints. Life between death and a new birth has been described in many different ways. Today our considerations will deal with much that has concerned me recently in the sphere of spiritual investigation.

We remember that as soon as we have gone through the gate of death we experience the kamaloca period during which we are still intimately connected with our feelings and emotions, with all the aspects of our soul life in the last earthly embodiment. We gradually free ourselves from this connection. Indeed, we no longer have a physical body after death. Yet, when the physical and etheric bodies have been laid aside, our astral body still possesses all the peculiarities it had on earth, and these peculiarities of the astral body, which it acquired because it lived in a physical body, also have to be laid aside. This requires a certain time and that marks the period of kamaloca. The kamaloca period is followed by experiences in the spiritual world or devachan. In our writings it has been characterized more from the aspect of what man experiences through the different elements spread out around him. We shall now consider the period between death and a new birth from another side. Let us begin with a general survey.

When man has gone through the gate of death he has the following experience. During life on earth he is enclosed within his skin, and outside is space with things and beings. This is not so after death. Our whole being expands and we feel that we are becoming ever larger. The feeling of being here in my skin with space and surrounding things out there is an experience that we do not have after death. After death we are inside objects and beings. We expand within a definite spatial area. During the kamaloca period we are continually expanding, and when this expansion reaches its end, we are as large as the space within the orbit of the moon. The fact of dwelling within space, of being concentrated in one point, has quite a different meaning after death than during physical existence. All the souls who dwell simultaneously in kamaloca fill out the same space circumscribed by the orbit of the moon. They interpenetrate one another. Yet this interpenetration does not mean togetherness. The feeling of being together is determined by quite other factors than filling a common spatial area. It is possible for two souls who are within the same space after death to be quite distant from one another. Their experience may be such that they need not know of one another's existence. Other souls, on the other hand, might have close, intimate connections and sense each other's presence. This depends entirely on inner relationships and has nothing to do with external spatial connections.

In later phases when kamaloca has come to an end, we penetrate into still vaster realms. We expand ever more. When the kamaloca phase draws to a close, man leaves behind him as if removed everything that during his physical existence was the expression of his propensities, longings and desires for earthly life. Man must experience all this but he must also relinquish it in the Moon sphere or kamaloca. As man lives on after death, and later recalls the experiences in the Moon sphere, he will find all his earthly emotions and passions inscribed there, that is, everything that developed in his soul life as a result of his positive attraction to the bodily nature. This is left behind in the Moon sphere and there it remains. It cannot be erased so easily. We carry it with us as an impulse but it remains inscribed in the Moon sphere. The account of the debts, as it were, owing by every person is recorded in the Moon sphere.

As we expand farther we enter a second realm that is called the Mercury sphere in occultism. We shall not represent it diagrammatically, but the Mercury sphere is larger than the Moon sphere. We enter this sphere after death in the most varied ways. It can be accurately investigated by means of spiritual science. A person who in life had an immoral or limited moral disposition lives into the Mercury sphere in a completely different way from one who was morally inclined. In the Mercury sphere the former is unable to find those people who die at the same time, shortly before or after he did, and who are also in the spiritual world. He so enters into the spiritual world that he is unable to find the loved ones with whom he longs to be together. People who lack a moral disposition of soul on earth become hermits in the Mercury sphere. The morally inclined person, however, becomes what one might call a sociable being. There he will find above all the people with whom he had a close inner connection on earth. This determines whether one is together with someone. It depends not on spatial relations, for we all fill the same space, but on our soul inclinations. We become hermits when we bring an unmoral disposition with us, and sociable beings, if we possess a moral inclination.

We encounter other difficulties in connection with sociability in the Moon sphere during kamaloca but by and large whether a man becomes a hermit or a sociable being there also depends on the disposition of his soul. A thoroughgoing egoist on earth, one who only indulged his urges and passions, will not easily find in the Moon sphere the people with whom he was connected on earth. A man who has loved passionately, however, even if it were only physically, will nevertheless not find himself completely alone, but will find other individuals with whom he was connected. In both these spheres it is generally not possible to find human beings apart from those with whom one has been connected on earth. Others remain unknown to us. The condition for meeting other people is that we must have been with them on earth. Whether or not we find ourselves with them depends on the moral factor. Although they lead to a connection with those we have known on earth, even moral strivings will not carry us much farther beyond this realm. Relationships to the people we meet after death are characterized by the fact that they cannot be altered.

We should picture it as follows. During life on earth we

always have the possibility of changing a relationship with a fellow man. Let us suppose that over a period of time we have not loved someone as he deserved. The moment we become aware of this we can love him rightly, if we have the strength. We lack this possibility after death. Then when we encounter a person we perceive far more clearly than on earth whether we have loved him too little or unfairly, but we can do nothing to change it. It has to remain as it is. Life connections bear the peculiar quality of a certain constancy. Because they are of a lasting nature, an impulse is formed in the soul by means of which order is brought into karma. If we have loved a person insufficiently over a period of fifteen years, we shall become aware of it after death. It is during our experience of this that we bring about the impulse to act differently in our next incarnation on earth. We thereby create the impulse and the will for karmic compensation. That is the technique of karma.

Above all, we should be clear about one thing. During the early phases of life after death, namely during the Moon and Mercury periods (and also during subsequent periods that will shortly be described), we dwell in the spiritual world in such a way that our spiritual life depends on how we lived on earth in the physical world. It not only is a question of our earthly consciousness. Our unconscious impulses also play a part. In our normal waking state on earth we live in our ego. Below the ego-consciousness lies the astral consciousness, the subconscious sphere. The workings of this sphere are sometimes different from our normal ego-consciousness without our being aware of it.

Let us take an actual example that occurs quite frequently. Two people are on the friendliest terms with each other. One develops an appreciation for spiritual science while the other, who previously appeared quite complacent towards it, comes to hate spiritual science. This animosity need not pervade the whole soul. It may only be lodged in the person's ego-consciousness, not in his astral consciousness. As far as his astral consciousness is concerned, the person who feeds his animosity still further might in fact have a longing and a love for the spirit of which he is unaware. That is quite possible. There are contradictions of this kind in human nature. If a person investigates his astral consciousness, his subconscious, he might well find a concealed sympathy for what in his waking consciousness he professes to hate. This is of particular importance after death because then, in this respect, man becomes truly himself. A person may have brought himself to hate spiritual science during a lifetime, to reject it and everything connected with it, and yet he may have a love for it in his subconscious. He may have a burning desire for spiritual science. The fact of not knowing and being unable to form thoughts of his memories can result in acute suffering during the period of kamaloca because during the first phase after death man lives mainly in his recollections. His existence is then not only determined by the sorrow and also the joy of what lives in his ego-consciousness. What has developed in the subconscious also plays a part. Thus man becomes truly as he really is.

Here we can see that spiritual science rightly understood is destined to work fruitfully in all spheres of life. A person who has gone through the gate of death is unable to bring about any change in his relation to those around him, and the same is true of the others in relation to him. An immutability in the connections has set in. But a sphere of change does remain that is in the relationship of the dead to the living. Inasmuch as they have had a relationship on earth with those who have died, the living are the only ones who can soothe the pain and alleviate the anguish of those who have gone through the gate of death. In many cases such as these, reading to the dead has proved fruitful.

A person has died. During his lifetime for one reason or another he did not concern himself with spiritual science. The one who remains behind on earth can know by means of spiritual science that the deceased has a burning thirst for spiritual science. Now if the one who remains behind concerns himself with thoughts of a spiritual nature as if the dead were there with him, he performs a great service to him. We can actually read to the dead. That enables the gulf that exists between the living and the dead to be bridged. The two worlds, the physical and the spiritual, are severed by materialism. Consider how their union will take hold of life itself! When spiritual science does not remain mere theory but becomes a life impulse as it should, there will not be separation but immediate communication. By reading to the dead we can enter in immediate connection with them and help them. The one who has avoided spiritual science will continue to feel the anguish of longing for it unless we help him. We can assist him from the earth if such a longing is at all present. By this means the living can help the dead.

It also is possible for the dead to be perceived by the living, although in our time the living do little to bring about such connections. Also in this respect spiritual science will take hold of life, will become a true life elixir. To understand in which way the dead can influence the living let us take the following as our starting point. What does man know about the world? Remarkably little if we only consider the things of the physical plane with mere waking consciousness. Man is aware of what happens out there in front of his senses and what he can construe by means of his intellect in relation to these happenings. Of all else he is ignorant. In general he believes that he cannot know anything apart from what he observes by means of sense perception. But there is much else that does not happen and yet is of considerable importance. What does this mean?

Let us assume that we are in the habit of going to work at eight o'clock every morning. On one occasion, however, we are delayed by five minutes. Apart from the fact that we arrive five minutes late, nothing unusual has happened apparently. Yet, upon closer consideration of all the elements involved, we might become aware that precisely on that day, if we had left at the correct time we would have been run over. That means that had we left at the right time we would no longer be alive.

Or what is also possible and might have occurred is that a person might have been prevented by a friend from sailing on the *Titanic*. He might feel that had he sailed he surely would have been drowned! That this was karmically planned is another matter. But do think, when you consider life in this way, of how little you are in fact aware. If nothing of what might have taken place has happened, then you are simply unaware of it. People do not pay attention to the countless possibilities that exist in the world of actual events.

You might say that surely this is of no importance. For the outer events it matters little, yet it is of importance that you were not killed. I would like to draw your attention to the fact that we might have known that there was a high probability of being killed if, for instance, we had not missed the train that was involved in a major accident. One cannot mention all possible cases and yet they happen constantly on a small scale. Certainly, for the external course of events we only need know what can be observed. Let us assume that we definitely know that something would have happened had we not missed the train. Such a knowledge makes an inner impression on us, and we might say that we have been saved in a remarkable way by good fortune. Consider the many possibilities that confront people. How much richer would our soul lives be if we could know all the things that play into life and yet do not happen! Today people only consider the poverty-stricken sequence of what has actually occurred.

It is as if one were to consider a field with its many ears of wheat and reflect that from it a relatively small number of seeds will be sown. Countless others will not sprout and will go in another direction. What might happen to us is related to what actually occurs as the many grains of wheat that do not sprout are related to those that sprout and carry ears. This is literally so, for the possibilities in life are infinite. Moments in which especially important things for us in the world of probability are taking place are also particularly favorable moments for the dead to draw near. Let us suppose that a person left five minutes early, and as a result his life was preserved. At a particular moment he was saved from an accident, or it might also happen that in such a manner a joyful event escaped him. A dream picture that imparts a message from the dead can enter life at such moments. But people live crudely. As a rule, the finer influences that constantly play into life go unheeded. In this respect, spiritual science refines the feelings and sensations. As a result, man will sense the influence of the dead and will experience a connection with him. The gulf between the living and the dead is bridged by spiritual science that becomes a true life elixir.

The next sphere after death is the so-called Venus sphere. In this sphere we become hermits if on earth we have had an irreligious disposition. We become sociable spirits if we bring a religious inclination with us. Inasmuch as in the physical world we are able to feel our devotion to the Holy Spirit, so in the Venus sphere shall we find all those of a like inclination towards the divine spiritual. Men are grouped according to religious and philosophic trends in the Venus sphere. On earth it is so that both religious striving and religious experience still play a dominant part. In the Venus sphere the grouping is purely according to religious confession and philosophic outlook. Those who share the same world-conception are together in large, powerful communities in the Venus sphere. They are not hermits. Only those are hermits who have not been able to develop any religious feeling and experience.

For instance, the monists, the materialists of our age, will not be sociable, but lonely beings. Each one will be as if encaged in the Venus sphere. There can be no question of a Monistic Union because by virtue of the monistic conception each member is condemned to loneliness. The fact that each is locked in his cage has not been thought out. It is mentioned so that souls may be brought to an awareness of reality as compared to the fanciful theories of monism that have been elaborated on earth. In general we can say that we come together with those of the same world-conception, of the same faith as ourselves. Other confessions are hard to understand in the Venus sphere.

This is followed by the Sun sphere. Only what bridges the differences between the various religious confessions can help us in the Sun sphere. People do not find it easy to throw bridges from one confession to another because they are so entrenched in their own views. A real understanding for one who thinks and feels differently is particularly difficult. In theory such an understanding is often claimed, but matters are quite different when it is a question of putting theory into practice.

One finds, for instance, that many who belong to the Hindu religion speak of a common kernel in all religions. They in fact, however, only refer to the common kernel of the Hindu and Buddhist religions. The adherents of the Hindu and Buddhistic religions speak in terms of a particular egoism. They are caught in a group egoism.

One might insert here a beautiful Estonian legend about group egoism that tells of the origin of languages. God wished to bestow the gift of language on humanity by means of fire. A great fire was to be kindled and the different languages were to come about by having men listen to the peculiarities of the sounds of the fire. So the Godhead called all the peoples of the earth to assemble so that each might learn its language. Prior to the gathering, however, God gave preference to the Estonians and taught them the divine-spiritual language, a loftier mode of speech. Then the others drew near and were allowed to listen to how the fire was burning, and as they heard it they learned to understand the various sounds. Certain peoples preferred by the Estonians came first when the fire was still burning quite strongly. When the fire was reaching its end the Germans had their turn, for the Estonians are not particularly fond of the Germans. In the feebly crackling fire one heard, "*Deitsch, peitsch; deitsch, peitsch*" (German, whip). Then followed the Lapps of whom the Estonians are even less fond. One only heard,

"Lappen latschen" (Lapp, lash). By that time the fire was reduced to mere ashes, and the Lapps brought forth the worst language of all because the Estonians and the Lapps are deadly enemies. Such is the extent of the Estonians' group egoism.

A similar group egoism is true of most peoples when they speak of penetrating to the essential core common to all religious creeds. In this respect Christianity is absolutely not the same as all the other creeds. If, for example, the attitude in the West was comparable to that toward the Hindu religion, then old Wotan still would reign as a national god. The West has not acknowledged a ruling divinity to be found within its own area, but one outside it. That is an important difference between it and Hinduism and Buddhism. In many respects, Western Christianity is not permeated by religious egoism. Religiously it is more selfless than the Eastern religions. This is also the reason why a true knowledge and experience of the Christ impulse can bring man to a right connection with his fellow men, irrespective of the confessions they acknowledge.

In the Sun sphere between death and rebirth it is really a matter of an understanding that enables us not only to come together with those of a like confession, but also to form a relationship with mankind as a whole. If sufficiently broadly understood in its connection with the Old Testament religion, Christianity is not one-sided. Attention has been drawn previously to something of considerable importance that should be recognized. You will recall that one of the most beautiful sayings of Christ, "Ye are Gods," is reminiscent of the Old Testament. Christ points to the fact that a divine spark, a god, dwells in every human being. You are all Gods; you will be on a par with the Gods.

It is a lofty teaching of Christ that points man to his divine nature, that he can become like God. You can become God-like, a wonderful and deeply moving teaching of Christ! Another being has used the same words, and it is indicative of the Christian faith that another being has done so. At the opening of the Old Testament Lucifer approaches man. He takes his starting point—and therein lies the temptation—with the words, "You shall be as Gods." Lucifer at the beginning of the temptation in Paradise and later Christ Jesus use the same words! We touch here upon one of the deepest and most important aspects of Christianity because this indicates that it is not merely a matter of the content of the words, but of which being in the cosmic context utters them. In the last Mystery Drama it had to be shown that the same words have a totally different meaning according to whether spoken by Lucifer, Ahriman or the Christ. We touch here upon a deep cosmic mystery, and it is important that we should develop an understanding for the words, "Ye are Gods" and "Ye shall be as Gods," uttered on one occasion by the Christ, on the other by Lucifer.

We must consider that between death and rebirth we also dwell in the Sun sphere where a thorough understanding of the Christ impulse is essential. We must bring this understanding along with us from the earth, for Christ once did dwell in the Sun but, as we know, He descended from the Sun and united Himself with the earth. We have to carry Him up to the Sun period, and then we can become sociable beings through the Christ impulse and learn to understand Him in the sphere of the Sun.

We must learn to discriminate between Christ and Lucifer, and in our time this is only possible by means of anthroposophy. The understanding of Christ that we bring with us from the earth leads us as far as the Sun sphere. There it acts as a guide, so to speak, from man to man, irrespective of creed or confession. But we encounter another being in the Sun sphere who utters words that have virtually the same content. That being is Lucifer. We must have acquired on earth an understanding of the difference between Christ and Lucifer, for Lucifer is now to accompany us through the further spheres between death and rebirth.

So you see, we go through the Moon, Mercury, Venus, and Sun spheres. In each sphere we meet, to begin with, what corresponds to the inner forces that we bring with us. Our emotions, urges, passions, sensual love, unite us to the Moon sphere. In the Mercury sphere we meet everything that is due to our moral imperfections; in the Venus sphere, all our religious shortcomings; in the Sun sphere, everything that severs us from the purely human.

Now we proceed to other spheres that the occultist terms the spheres of Mars, Jupiter and Saturn. Here Lucifer is our guide and we enter into a realm that bestows new forces upon us. Just as here we have the earth below us, so there in the cosmos we have the Sun below us. We grow into the divine-spiritual world, and as we do so we must hold fast in memory what we have brought with us of the Christ impulse. We can only acquire this on earth and the more deeply we have done so, the farther we can carry it into the cosmos. Now Lucifer draws near to us. He leads us out into a realm we must cross in order to be prepared for a new incarnation. There is one thing we cannot dispense with unless Lucifer is to become a threat to us, and that is the understanding of the Christ impulse, of what we have heard about Christ during our life on earth. Lucifer approaches us out of his own accord during the period between birth and death, but Christ must be received during earthly life.

We then grow into the other spheres beyond the Sun. We become ever larger, so to speak. Below us we have the Sun and above, the mighty, vast expanse of the starry heavens. We grow into the great cosmic realm up to a certain boundary, and as we grow outward cosmic forces work upon us from all directions. We receive forces from the mighty world of the stars into our widespread being.

We reach a boundary, then we begin to contract and enter again into the realms through which we have travelled previously. We go through the Sun, Venus, Mercury, and Moon spheres until we come again into the neighborhood of the earth and everything that has been carried out in the cosmic expanse has concentrated itself again in an embryo borne by an earthly mother.

That is the mystery of man's nature between death and a new birth. After he has gone through the gate of death he expands ever more from the small space of the earth to the realms of Moon, Mercury, Venus, Sun, Mars, Jupiter and Saturn. We have then grown into cosmic space, like giant spheres. After we as souls have received the forces of the universe, of the stars, we contract again and carry the forces of the starry world within us. This explains out of spiritual science how in the concentrated brain structure an imprint of the total starry heavens may be found. In fact, our brain does contain an important secret.

We have yet another mystery. Man has gathered himself together, incarnated in a physical body to which he comes by way of his parents. He has journeyed so far during his expansion in cosmic space that he has recorded his particular characteristics there. As we gaze from the earth upward to the heavens, there are not only stars but also our characteristics from previous incarnations. If, for instance, we were ambitious in previous earth lives, then this ambition is recorded in the starry world. It is recorded in the Akasha Chronicle, and when you are here on the earth at a particular spot, this ambition comes to you with the corresponding planet in a certain position and makes its influence felt.

That accounts for the fact that astrologers do not merely consider the stars and their motions but will tell you that here is your vanity, there is your ambition, your moral failing, your indolence; something you have inscribed into the stars is now working out of the starry worlds onto the earth and determines your destiny. What lives in our souls is recorded in the vastness of space and it works back from space during our life on earth as we journey here between birth and death. If we truly understand them, these matters touch us closely, and they enable us to explain many things.

I have concerned myself a great deal with Homer. Last summer during my investigations into the conditions between death and rebirth I came upon the immutability of the connections after death. Here, in a particular passage, I had to say to myself that the Greeks called Homer the blind poet because he was such a great seer. Homer mentions that life after death takes place in a land where there is no change. A wonderfully apt description! One only learns to understand this through the occult mysteries. The more one strives in this direction, the more one realizes that the ancient poets were the greatest seers and that much that is secretly interwoven in their works requires a considerable amount of understanding.

I would like to mention something that happened to me last autumn and which is quite characteristic. At first, I resisted it because it was so astonishing, but it is one of those cases where objectivity wins. In Florence we find the tombs of Lorenzo and Giuliano de Medici by Michelangelo. The two brothers are portrayed together with four allegorical figures. These figures are well known, but at a first visit it occurred to me that something was not quite right with this group. It was clear to me that the one described as Giuliano is Lorenzo, and vice versa. The figures, which can be removed, had obviously been interchanged on some occasion and it has gone unheeded. That is why the statue of Giuliano is said to be that of Lorenzo, and vice versa. But I am really concerned here with the four allegorical figures.

Let us first deal with this wonderful statue, "Night." It cannot be understood simply in terms of an allegory. If, however, knowing about the etheric body and imagining it in its full activity, one were to ask, "What is the most characteristic gesture corresponding to the etheric body when it is free from the astral body and ego?" the answer would be the gesture as given by Michelangelo in "Night." In fact, "Night" is so molded that it gives a perfect representation of the free, independent etheric body, expressed by means of the forms of the physical body when the astral body and ego are outside it. This figure is not an allegory, but represents the combination of the physical and etheric bodies when the astral body and ego are outside them. Then one understands the position of the figure. It is historically the truest expression of the vitality of the etheric body.

One comes to see the figure of "Day" as the expression of the ego when it is most active and least influenced by the astral, etheric and physical bodies. This is portrayed in the strange gesture and position of Michelangelo's "Day." We obtain the gesture of the figure "Dawn" when the astral body is active, independent from the physical and etheric bodies and the ego, and of "Dusk" when the physical body is active without the other three members.

I struggled long against this piece of knowledge and to begin with thought it quite absurd; yet the more one goes into it, the more it compels one to recognize the truth of the script contained in these sculptures. It is not that Michelangelo was conscious of it. It sprang from his intuitive creative power. One also understands the meaning of the legend that tells that when Michelangelo was alone in his studio, the figure "Night" became endowed with life, and would move around freely. It is a special illustration of the fact that one is dealing with the etheric body. The spirit works into everything in art as in the evolution of humanity. One learns to understand the world of the senses only if one grasps how the spirit works into sensible reality.

There is a beautiful saying by Kant. He says, "There are two things that have made a specially deep impression on me, the starry heavens above me and the moral law within me." It is particularly impressive when we realize that both are really one and the same. Between death and rebirth we are spread out over the starry realms and receive their forces into ourselves, and during our life in a physical body the forces we have gathered are active within us as moral impulses. Looking up to the starry heavens we may say that we dwell among the forces that are active out there during the period between death and rebirth. This now becomes the guiding principle of our moral life. The starry heavens outside and the moral law within are one and the same reality. They constitute two sides of that reality. We experience the starry realms between death and rebirth, the moral law between birth and death.

When we grasp this, spiritual science grows into a mighty prayer. For what is a prayer but that which links our soul with the divine-spiritual permeating the world. We must make it our own as we go through the experiences of the world of the senses. Inasmuch as we strive consciously towards this goal, what we learn becomes a prayer of its own accord. Here spiritual knowledge is transformed immediately into feeling and experience, and that is how it should be. However much spiritual science might work with concepts and ideas, they will nevertheless be transformed into pure sensations and prayer-like feelings. That is what our present time requires. Our time needs to experience the cosmos by living into a consideration of the spirit in which the study itself takes on the nature of a prayer. Whereas the study of the external physical world becomes ever more dry, scholarly and abstract, the study of spiritual life will become more heartfelt and deeper. It will take on the quality of prayer, not in a one-sided sentimental sense but by virtue of its own nature. Then man will not know merely as a result of abstract ideas that the divine that permeates the universe is also in him. He will realize as he advances in knowledge that he truly has experienced it during life between the last death and a new birth. He will know that what he experienced then is now in him as the inner riches of his life.

Such considerations, related as they are to recent research, help us to gain an understanding of our own development. Then spiritual science will be able to transform itself into a true spiritual life blood. We shall often speak further about these matters in the future.

BETWEEN DEATH AND A NEW BIRTH

Vienna, January 21, 1913

VIII

BETWEEN DEATH AND A NEW BIRTH

Vienna, January 21, 1913

THE LAST time I spoke to you here, I dealt briefly with a significant phase of human life between death and rebirth. This phase cannot be treated as if it were of no importance for our physical existence. We should be clear about the fact that the forces we need for life do not only come from the realm of the physical body. They emanate essentially from a supersensible world to which we belong between death and rebirth. This can be understood only if we are able to form mental images of life between death and rebirth.

Man is mostly enveloped in a kind of dreaming-sleeping condition. Those who go through the daily routine without thinking about the events they experience are in fact asleep to life, and those who concern themselves with what lies beyond material existence are also those who awaken to physical life. Referring to our earlier considerations, you will remember that spiritual science rightly understood is capable of entering fully into all aspects of human existence. Inasmuch as spiritual science permeates our civilization, humanity will experience an awakening from a sleep of life. Many things that approach the human being appear strange and mysterious, but they represent a riddle

149

more to the feelings than to the dry intellect. A mother standing by the coffin of her child, or the reverse, is such an instance. One has but to concern oneself thoroughly with human existence to realize how people become aware of the riddle of life. People who have lost a sister, a husband, or a wife come to me and say, "I never used to think about death, never concerned myself about what might happen afterwards, but since this relative has been taken from me it is as if he were still here, and this has led me to occupy myself with spiritual science." Life will bring people to spiritual science. What happens as a result will be richly rewarding because spiritual science can permeate life with certain impulses that it alone can give.

When a person is no longer physically present, the riddle arises as to what happens to him after death. External science cannot supply the answer because it only observes with the eyes, and they, too, decay. The physical brain decays also, and it is clear that it can be of no use for what man experiences without his physical sheath. Yet the mighty questions regarding the beyond remain. In this connection general answers are of little avail and it is preferable to consider actual instances that can penetrate directly into life.

Let us take life on earth as a starting point. Perhaps you will have come across a person who, through a deep inner longing, through his own soul disposition, was driven to spiritual science, whereas another may have become antagonistic towards it. The one became more deeply involved in spiritual science, while his friend developed increasing enmity towards it. Life not only presents us with a maya in nature but also in the immediacy of our connection with others. In fact, what has just been related may be a complete deception. He who has convinced himself that all this is nonsense may, in the depths of his soul of which he remains unconscious, develop a secret love for it. In the substrata love can express itself as hate. One does find such cases in earthly life. When a person has gone through the gate of death, all the secret soul impulses and longings that he has suppressed during his earthly existence rise to the surface and become the content of the period of catharsis. We have observed people going through the gate of death who on earth were enemies of spiritual science and who after death developed an intensive longing for it. Such antagonists then strive for spiritual science. Had we during their earthly lives gone to them with a book on spiritual science, they might have dismissed us in anger. After death we can do them no greater service than to read to them. Reading in thought to the dead can have the greatest furthering effect for them.

There are many instances within our spiritual movement in which those connected with a dead person have read to him and thereby helped him. The dead receive what is given with the utmost gratitude, and in this way a beautiful relationship can be developed. This shows what spiritual science can mean quite practically. Spiritual science is not mere theory. It must take hold of life and tear down the wall that separates the living from the dead. Thus can the gulf be bridged. A great deal of good can be done by bringing spiritual science into life with the right attitude. No better advice can be given than to read to the dead because it is a strange fact that immediately after death we are incapable of making new connections. We are forced to continue with the old ones.

The question presents itself as to whether or not the

dead are able to find spiritual beings beyond the threshold who could teach them. That is not possible! To begin with, one can only have connections with beings with whom one has had a relationship before going through the gate of death. On encountering a being one has not known on earth, one merely passes him by. On earth, too, one would not recognize a great genius if he were dressed like a teamster. One has contact only with the individuals one has known on earth. One might meet many beings who could be of help, but if there has been no prior connection, they can be of no use to one. Spiritual science is in its early stages and because it has only just begun to have an effect on human beings, the living can perform the greatest service to the dead by helping them in this way. This is an instance of the influence that can be exercised from our world upon the other. But the opposite is also possible—the dead can work into the physical world. To the extent that spiritual science takes hold of life, a cooperation between both worlds will come about. The dead can also influence the living.

People know remarkably little about the world. At most, only what happens in the course of time is grasped. Many think that the rest is of no significance. But what actually occurs is only the smallest part of what is worth knowing. By knowing only what happens externally, one actually remains ignorant of life. In the morning we go to work. Probably we consider the things that happen there as well worth knowing. One day we leave three minutes later than usual and surprising events take place. If, for example, we had left home at the right time we might have been run over, but we have been protected. Or perhaps we have to make a trip and miss the train. Then this very train is involved in a serious accident. What can we gather from such considerations?

There is much that does not happen in life, and yet we should reckon such events among the possibilities. Does the individual know how many such possibilities he escapes every single day? Imagine all the things that could happen from which he is protected! We overlook them because for a cold, abstract view of life they are quite meaningless. But let us consider the effect on the soul of a person who has been saved from danger by an apparent coincidence. A man from Berlin intended to go to America and had already purchased his ticket. A friend advised him not to sail on the *Titanic*! Picture to yourself the feelings of this man. He did not sail, and then he heard of the sinking of the *Titanic*. It had a shattering effect on his feelings. What impressions would arise in us if we were able to observe in the course of the day all the things we have been spared! When a person begins to concern himself with spiritual science he develops a far greater sensitivity for the complexities of life, for what happens in the normal course of the day.

Now if we have acquired a sensitivity of soul and are spiritually prepared, at moments such as these we can receive an impression from the spiritual world, a message from the dead that comes as an act of grace. The gates are flung open by the dead. They can speak to those who have developed sensitivity. Important matters can be imparted. The dead person, for example, may order us to accomplish something that he has not done. So the gulf is bridged. When spiritual science penetrates into practical life, and it will do so in the future, we shall be able to communicate in both directions with the dead. It will bring the supersensible world into the immediate present.

The following question may arise. When we read a spiritual-scientific book in a particular language, can the dead understand this language? During the period of catharsis the dead understand the language they have spoken on earth. It is only later, during the passage into devachan, that they can no longer understand words but only thoughts. A transformation in the intercourse with the dead takes place after a definite period of years. If the one who has remained on earth is sensitive, he will feel that the one who has died is with him and that they think the same. This can last for years and then suddenly one loses the connection. That is the moment when the dead passes into devachan. During the period of catharsis he still remembers earthly life, he still holds onto these memories.

What is an earthly language? Every language has meaning only for earthly life and is closely connected with a person's organization, with the climate and with the formation of the larynx. In Europe we do not speak the same languages as in India. But thoughts are not bound to the physical organization; thoughts are not formed according to earthly conditions. The dead only understand language as long as they are in kamaloca. When a medium conveys a message from the dead in a particular language, it can only come from one who has recently gone through the gate of death.

Fundamentally we are already within the higher worlds every time we go to sleep, for in sleep we enter unconsciously the same realm we enter after death.

I would like to pose the following question. Can someone who is not yet able to see with supersensible perception nevertheless know about these things? A sleeping man, of course, does live. He is somewhat like a plant. You may recall that a scientist, Raoul Francé, writes that plants are endowed with feelings and are able to admire. Yet plants do not have a soul element. The sleeping human organism is on par with the plant. The rays of the sun have to fall on the plant if it is to live. The earth is covered with plants because the sun has called them forth. Without the sun there are no plants and during the winter they cannot sprout forth.

When man sleeps, where is his sun? What lies in the bed we also cannot envisage without the sun. This sun is outside the man's ego. There the ego has to work on the sleeping organism as the sun does on the plant. But it is not only the sun that plays a part in bringing forth and sustaining vegetation. The moon does also. Without the influences from the moon there would be no plant growth either, but the effect of lunar influences is completely ignored by scientists.

The light of the moon influences the plant. The lunar forces determine the width of a plant. A plant that grows tall and thin is little influenced by the moon. Even the whole cosmos is involved in the growth of plants. The ego works into the physical and etheric bodies as the sun influences plant growth. Similarly, the astral body is related to the moon. The ego is the sun for the physical body, the astral body is spiritually its moon. Our ego creates a replacement for the influences of the sun, and our astral body for those of the moon. This justifies what the initiate means when he says man has been formed as an extract of the forces of the cosmos. As the sun is the central point of the plant world and rays forth its light in all directions, in the same way light must permeate the physical and etheric bodies. The sunlight is not only physical, it is also of a soul-spiritual nature separated from the cosmos and become the "I" or ego. The human astral body contains an extract of the light of the moon. The greatest wisdom is contained in these matters.

If the human ego were still bound to the sun, man would only be able to alternate between sleeping and waking like the plants. If there were only the solar influence we would never be able to sleep during the day. We would sleep only at night. But our whole cultural life depends upon an emancipation from these conditions. We carry our own sun within us and the ego is an extract of the solar influence. The astral body in man is an extract of the lunar influence. So during sleep we are not dependent in the spiritual world on the cosmic solar influence. Our ego does what the sun would do otherwise. We are illumined by our own ego and astral body.

Ancient occult vision penetrated to this point only occasionally. Spiritual science gives us the following picture of the sleeping man. Above him shines the sun, his ego, without which he could not be as a plant during sleep. Above him shines the moon, his own astral body.

Now, we can also picture that during the autumn when the sun's influence decreases, vegetation withers. In a man who is awake the astral body and ego are within the physical and ether bodies. The return into the body is to a certain extent like the setting of the sun and moon, and it also marks the end of the plant-like existence. The vegetative condition that prevails to revivify our forces during sleep is much less active during waking life. The vegetative growth-forces wane as man awakens. Inasmuch as we are plant-like, we die every morning. This throws considerable light on the interplay between soul and body. Some people feel active and stimulated shortly after waking. Those are the ones who are able to live more strongly in the soul sphere. People who tend to live more in the bodily nature often sense a certain fatigue in the morning. The less tired a person is in the morning, the more active he can be. Yet our waking life may be compared to the dying process of the plants in winter. Each day we draw death forces within our organism. They accumulate and because of this process we eventually die. The fundamental reason for death lies in the sphere of consciousness. From this we can gather that the conscious activity of the ego within our daily life is the destroyer of our physical and etheric bodies. We die because we live consciously.

Many attempts are being made to explain the nature of sleep. Sleep is supposed to be a condition of exhaustion and is said to exist to dispel tiredness. But sleep is not really a condition of exhaustion. The small child, for instance, sleeps more than anyone. Sleep is a part of the whole of life. It is inserted in the rhythm of falling asleep and waking up. Similarly, as we see nature wither in winter, so something dies in us during our waking life.

When we go through the gate of death, we leave our physical and etheric bodies behind and our ego and astral body now emerge as sun and moon that have nothing to illumine. Nevertheless, the ego and the astral body can continue their existence in spite of the fact that they have nothing to illumine. When they permeate the body, consciousness arises. In the spiritual world also, man has to permeate something if he is to acquire consciousness, otherwise he would exist without consciousness.

Into what does man enter after death? He plunges into spiritual substance that is present without earthly participation. Since the Mystery of Golgotha man must always penetrate into the Christ-substance of the earth that has come about through the deed on Golgotha. We have learned to know the Christ as the Sun Spirit. The ego has emancipated itself from the light of the sun. Then the mighty Sun Spirit descended to the earth, and thereby does the ego of man penetrate into the substance of the Sun Spirit. Man experiences this plunging into the Christ-substance when he has gone through the gate of death. Because of this he is able to develop consciousness after death. In nature this stage will be accomplished when the earth has reached the Vulcan condition. As the sun shines from above downward on the earth, it conjures forth the carpet of vegetation. Now assume the sun were to shine on the earth with sufficient strength to bring forth plants, but the earth was unable to bring them forth and instead reflected the sunlight back. Then the sunlight would not be lost but would shine out into cosmic space and bring forth a supersensible vegetation. This does in fact occur, not physically but spiritually. Because the Christ united Himself with the earth every individual who has united himself with the Christ is able to experience after death the repercussions of what he has grasped consciously on earth. Thus we can understand that on *earth* man must acquire the capacity to develop consciousness after death. He must carry over from his physical body the forces that develop consciousness.

The bodily nature was most strongly illumined during the Greco-Latin period. Then the saying, "Rather a beggar on earth than a king in the realm of the Shades," had reality. At that time to dwell in the underworld meant to lead a miserable existence. Before the birth of Christ life after death was little developed. We, on the other hand, belong to an age that is characterized by the fact that such forces are no longer exercised on the bodily nature. Man, inasmuch as he sleeps, is on the decline. The bodily nature has been on the downgrade since the time of Christ. The vegetative forces were most strongly prevalent during the Greek epoch. At the end of the evolution of humanity the bodily nature will be most barren. In earlier epochs men were clairvoyant and the soul was highly developed. Through the soul-spiritual decline the bodily nature rose to its peak as expressed in the beauty of Greek art. But as we go into the future all striving for beauty is faced with a pitfall in that external beauty has no future. Beauty must become an inner quality and in this way must it reveal its character.

Insofar as this withering process increases, the inner nature of the sun and of the moon will become ever more glorious. Those who cultivate spirit and soul through spiritual science have a greater understanding of the future than those people who seek to revive the Greek games. The more a person leaves his soul-spiritual nature in unconsciousness, the more miserable is the destiny he will encounter between death and a new birth. The decay of the body has nothing to do with life after death, but if nothing of a soul-spiritual nature has been developed, then there is nothing to carry over into the spiritual world. The more a person has opened himself to receive a spiritual content, the better he will fare after death. Mankind will learn increasingly to become independent of what is bound to the physical body.

Spiritual science will not keep its present form. Words can scarcely express what it wishes to convey. In spiritual science more will depend on *how* things are said, rather than on *what* is said. That is an international element and can live in any language. One will accustom oneself to listen to *how* things are expressed. In this way one can enter into contact with the dwellers of devachan. Today we are gathered together and speak of spiritual science. We will go through the gate of death and continue to develop in a number of future incarnations. Then we will have thoughts independent from the earth-bound language of today. The spirit will enter into our life and we will be able to communicate with the dead.

External cultural life goes to its downfall. A time will come when the skies will be filled with airplanes. Life on earth will wither, but the human soul will grow into the spiritual world. At the end of earth evolution man will have progressed so that there will no longer be a sharp division between the living and the dead. The earth will go over into a spiritual condition again because man will have spiritualized himself. This will give you a basis for a correct answer when people ask, "Death and birth repeat themselves but will this always continue?" There will not be such a difference between living and dying because for human consciousness everything will be spiritualized. The upward development of the whole of mankind leads to the condition that will be experienced on Jupiter.

In speaking about life between death and rebirth we open up a far-reaching realm. There, also, everything is subject to change and transformation, including the intercourse of the living with the dead. We shall gradually penetrate further into the nature of man's existence, into the interplay between his bodily and spiritual nature.

LIFE AFTER DEATH

Linz, January 26, 1913

IX

LIFE AFTER DEATH

Linz, January 26, 1913

Wᴴᴬᵀ are our aims when we gather for spiritual-scientific studies? Many ask this question because those who are connected with spiritual science devote a part of their forces to considerations that for others actually do not come in question today. Truly, we consider realms that for the majority of people simply do not exist. Yet the gathering for such work is not merely the pursuit of an "ideal" in the sense of other ideals that are prevalent in our time.

The spiritual-scientific "ideal" is different in that it seeks to answer the call, which in our time is perhaps only heard faintly and by a few but which will become more and more audible in the world. Today there are some who are able to say clearly that spiritual science is a necessity and others do so out of indeterminate feeling. But out of what depths of the soul does this arise? Surely the one follows more or less what may be termed a spiritual instinct, an urge, that he is quite unable to bring to full consciousness. Yet such an urge corresponds to a rightly directed will. This may be observed when we investigate the soul life.

It is my intention on this occasion not to unfold general

theories but to deal with actual instances. This is especially necessary if we wish to answer the above question.

The seer who is able to look into the spiritual worlds also gradually gains an insight into the life between death and rebirth. This existence takes place in spiritual realms that are continually surrounding us, to which we belong with the best part of our soul life. Man lives purely in the spiritual world when he has gone through the gate of death and has laid aside his physical body. As long as he makes use of the physical senses and the intellect, the spiritual world remains hidden from him. The seer, however, can follow the different stages of life between death and rebirth.

The basic questions, which are important in relation to our ideals, do in fact stem from a consideration of life between death and a new birth. One might easily suppose that that life has nothing whatever to do with our life here on the physical plane, but in a deeper sense they are closely related. We become especially aware of this when we look at a soul that has gone through the gate of death. Let us take an actual instance and consider the relationship of such a soul to those who are still in a physical body.

A man went through the gate of death and left his wife and children behind. After a certain period had elapsed, it was possible for one able to look into the spiritual worlds to find this soul and a painful existence was revealed. The soul lamented the loss of wife and children. This expressed itself approximately in the following words, but we should remember that the earthly words used to express what a soul seeks to convey are only an approximation and are similar to a garment. One naturally cannot convey the language of the dead by means of earthly words. It is different and one has to translate it.

So this soul lamented, "I used to live with those whom I have left behind. Previously when I dwelt in a physical body and would come home in the evening after I had done my work, I would join them, and what shone from their souls was like the light of the sun. Everything that I experienced in their company used to alleviate the burden of physical existence. I was then quite unable to imagine life in the physical world without my wife and children. I am able to recall our life together as it used to be in every detail. But when I awoke in the spiritual world after death, I was unable to find my wife and children. For me they are not there. Only memories remain. I know that they are below on the earth, but their soul life as it is taking place in thinking, feeling and willing from morning until night is as if extinguished. I am unable to find my loved ones however hard I try."

This is a genuine experience, and it is shared by many souls who cross the gate of death in our present time. It was not always so in the evolution of humanity. In ancient times it was different. Men crossed the threshold of death in another way but they also were not in their physical bodies on earth as they are today.

The difference lies in the fact that in earlier times man still possessed a spiritual heritage by means of which he was linked to the spiritual world. The farther back we go in ancient periods when souls who are incarnate today were already present on the earth, the more we discover that man then was rightly connected to the spiritual world. Man has lost increasingly the old spiritual inheritance, and today we live in a period when there is a radical change in the evolution of humanity.

Let us clarify this point before embarking on the pro-

165

found facts previously described. In our time there are people who know little more about the starry heavens, for instance, than what is common knowledge today. True, there are still some who go out on a clear night and delight in the grandeur and glory of the starry heavens, but such people are in a minority. There are more and more people who are unable to distinguish between a planet and a fixed star but that is not the most important thing. Even when people do go out to look up to the heavens, they only see stars externally in their physical appearance. This was not the case in ancient times. It was not so for souls who are here today but who in ancient times dwelt in other bodies. The same souls who now see only the physical stars formerly beheld, when they contemplated the starry heavens, not so much the physical light of the stars but what was spiritually connected with them. Spiritual beings are connected with all the stars. What we term the higher hierarchies in spiritual science today were seen clairvoyantly by the souls of primeval times—by all of you here and by all the people outside. Man then did not merely see the physical world but he also beheld the spiritual world. It would have been sheer foolishness in those times to deny the spiritual world, as much as if today a person would deny the existence of roses and lilies. The spiritual world could not be denied because it was perceived. That man has lost the immediate connection with the spiritual world marks, in a certain sense, a step forward. In its place he has gained a greater degree of independence and freedom.

In former times the human soul lived in an external spiritual world. This realm gradually has been lost but the loss has to be replaced from within. Therefore, today the soul that relies merely on the perception of the outer world feels barren and empty. How many souls are there in our time who go about in the world totally oblivious of the fact that all space is filled by the presence of spiritual beings! One nevertheless can gain an understanding of the content of the spiritual by beholding the external world only. This is possible by penetrating into the depth of the soul. Many people, however, are not willing to do so, including the family of whom I spoke to you earlier.

The man in question dwelt in the spiritual world, in the realm in which we live between death and rebirth. He longed to be reunited with the souls with whom he had lived on earth, but for him they were not existent. Why? Because the souls who remained behind on the earth did not seek a spiritual content, because they were only able to manifest their presence by way of a physical body. He longed to know something of these souls who formerly had been to him as rays of sunshine, and the seer who was acquainted with him before he passed through the gate of death was not even able to comfort him in any special way. For comfort such as the following would have been fundamentally dishonest. "The souls that are extinguished for you will join you later if you have but the patience to wait. Then you will have them again as they were on earth." That would not have been quite true, because these souls were far removed from any form of penetration into spiritual life. They, too, after they have gone through the gate of death will have a fearful longing to be united with those whom they knew on earth. Souls who are devoid of any form of spiritual life encounter many obstacles.

We have reached the stage in the cycle of evolution of mankind when souls dwelling in a physical body must learn the language of the spirit. We must acquire a knowledge of higher worlds here. Many souls in our time despise a knowledge that may be termed theosophy in the literal sense of the word. This is truly the language that we must be able to speak after death if we wish to be rightly there for the spiritual world. After death we cannot make up for what we should have learned as the language of theosophy or spiritual science.

If the man I referred to had occupied himself with spiritual science together with his family, he would have had quite other experiences, another form of consciousness after death. In fact, he would have known that souls can be experienced there. Even if he was separated from them by a gulf they would one day join him. They would be able to find each other because they shared a common spiritual language. Otherwise he would not be reunited with them as one rightly should be after death. He would only encounter them as one meets people on earth who are dumb, who want to convey something but are quite incapable of doing so.

Truly it must be admitted that such facts are uncomfortable, and many of our contemporaries do not find them to their liking, but it is the truth that matters, not whether they sound pleasant or not.

In earlier periods of human evolution souls received much because they were still in their infancy and accepted religious traditions and ideas about the spiritual world in a childlike manner. As a result, they possessed a language for the spiritual life and were able to live in communion with spiritual beings. Now man is called upon, particularly in our age, to become ever more independent in his relation to spiritual life.

Spiritual science has not come into the world in an arbitrary way. It cannot be propagated by the means usually available and as is commonly the practice of societies that seek to spread their particular aims.

Those who feel called upon to carry spiritual ideas into our contemporary cultural life have experienced the painful cry of souls after death who are unable to find the ones they have left behind because spiritually they are empty. The cry of the dead is the call that brings forth the ideal of spiritual science.

One who is able to experience by entering into the spiritual world the agony, the longing, the renunciation, but also the hopelessness that fills the souls who have passed through the gate of death, knows the reason for our gatherings. He also knows that he cannot do otherwise than to represent this spiritual life. This is a matter of the greatest seriousness and it is called forth by the deepest longings of humanity.

Today there are souls who feel, even if out of the deepest recesses of their instincts that they wish to experience something of the spiritual world! They are the pioneers of a future when souls will come who will consider it important to cultivate a spiritual life founded on the cognition of the spiritual worlds. Spiritual life must be cultivated on earth in the sense of the new spiritual science, because otherwise humanity will increasingly enter into the other world spiritually dumb, lacking the capacity to open itself rightly.

It is also a fallacy to believe that we can wait until we have crossed the threshold of death to experience something of a spiritual nature over there. In order to experience anything of this kind one must have attained the faculty to perceive. But this faculty cannot be developed after death unless one has first acquired it here on earth. We do not live in vain in the material world! It is not for nothing that our souls descend to the physical world. They descend so that we may acquire what actually can only be acquired here, namely, spiritual cognition.

We cannot regard the earth as a mere vale of despair into which our souls are transposed, so to speak. We should consider the earth as a place by means of which we can acquire the possibility of developing spirituality. This is the truth of it.

If we question the seer further regarding the nature of life after death, he will reply that it is quite different from the course of life on earth. Here we travel across the world; we see the heavenly vault spread out above us, the sun that is shining. We look out and see the mountains, the lakes, the creatures of the various kingdoms of nature. We go through the world and carry our thoughts, sensations, passions, desires within us. Then we pass through the gate of death, but there things are different. For those unfamiliar with spiritual scientific observation, it all appears most paradoxical. What Schopenhauer said is correct, that "poor truth" must bear the fact that it is paradoxical.

The thoughts and mental images that we regard as belonging to an inner realm appear to us after death as our external world. After death all our thoughts and mental representations appear as a mighty panorama before the soul. People who go through life thoughtlessly travel through the world between death and rebirth in such a way that what should be experienced as filled with wisdom and thought content appears to them as empty and barren. Only they feel filled with a content between death and a new birth who have acquired the faculty to behold the thoughts spread out in the starry realms. One acquires this faculty between birth and death by evolving a thought content within the soul.

If we have not filled our soul here on earth with what the physical senses can give us, it is as if we were to journey along the path from death to rebirth like one who has no ears and therefore cannot hear a sound, like one who has no eyes and cannot perceive a single color. The sun in the heavens illuminates everything, but when it sets the surroundings disappear from our view. Likewise, things that are external in life appear after death as an inner world.

Let us consider what is yet another real experience to the seer. When we contemplate people who live between death and rebirth and seek to translate into our language what torments them, they tell us the following. "Something lives in me that causes me to suffer. It rises up out of my own self. It is akin to a headache in the physical world, except that the pain is experienced inwardly. I am myself the one who causes the pain." A human being after death may complain of much inner pain, inner suffering.

Now if the seer traces the origin of the inner suffering that strikes souls after death, he discovers that it comes from the way of life of these people here on earth. Suppose a person has felt a quite unjustifiable loathing for a fellow human being. Then the one who hated experiences inner pain after death, and he now suffers inwardly what he has inflicted on the other.

Whereas our thinking enables us to behold an outer world after death, so what we experience on earth as our external moral world, as the feeling relationships to other people, becomes our inner world after death. Indeed, it sounds grotesque and yet it is true that just as here we can feel a pain in our lungs, our stomach or our head, so after death a moral injustice can hurt. What is inner here is external there, and what is external here is inner there. We have reached the stage in the development of humanity when much can be experienced only after death.

A person who is not prepared to admit the reality of karma, of repeated earth lives, can never really accept the fact that a destiny belongs to him. How does a person go through the world? One person does this to him, the other that; he likes the one, dislikes the other. He does not know that he himself is the cause of what comes to meet him, of the painful experience inflicted by another person. This does not occur to him, for otherwise he would feel, "You have brought it on yourself!"

If during one's lifetime one is able to entertain such thoughts, then one at least will have a feeling as to the origin of the suffering one has to endure after death.

To know about karma in life between death and rebirth alleviates the pain, for otherwise the agonizing question as to why one has to suffer remains unanswered. In our time we have to begin to be aware of such things for without knowledge of them the evolution of humanity will not be able to continue.

Another instance is revealed to the seer. There are people who, between death and rebirth, are made to fulfill most unpleasant tasks. We should not imagine that we have nothing to do between death and a new birth. We have to accomplish the most varied tasks according to our individual capabilities. The seer finds, for instance, that there are souls who are forced to serve a being such as Ahriman after death.

As soon as we enter the realm beyond the physical, Ahriman appears quite clearly to us as a special being. Everything that has been portrayed as the domain of Ahriman and Lucifer in the drama, *The Guardian of the Threshold,* is real. Ahriman has a number of tasks to perform. The seer discovers souls who are appointed in the realm of Ahriman and have to serve that being. Why have they been condemned to serve Ahriman? The seer investigates how such people lived between birth and death, considers the principal characteristics of such souls, and discovers that they all suffered from one common evil, the love of ease. Love of ease and comfort are among the most widespread characteristics of contemporary humanity.

If we should inquire the reason that most people fail to do something, the answer invariably is, love of ease! Whether we turn our attention to the most important things of life or to mere trifles, love of ease permeates them all. To hold onto the old, not being able to shake it off, is a form of ease. In this respect people are not as bad as one is inclined to believe. It was not out of bad will that Giordano Bruno and Savanarola were burned at the stake or that Galileo was maltreated as he was. It is also not out of badness that great spirits are not appreciated during their lifetime, but rather out of love of ease! A long time has to elapse before people are able to think and feel along new lines, and it is only because of a love of ease! Love of ease and comfort are widespread characteristics, and it makes it possible to be enlisted after death into the ranks of Ahriman, for Ahriman, apart from his other functions, is the spirit of obstacles. Wherever obstacles arise Ahriman is master. He applies the brakes to life and to human beings.

Those who are subject to love of ease on earth will become agents to the slowing down process of everything that comes into the world from the supersensible. So love of ease fetters human souls between death and rebirth to spirits who, under Ahriman, are compelled to serve the powers of opposition and hindrance.

In many people we find a propensity that in everyday life we denote as an immoral characteristic, and that is lack of conscience. In the voice of conscience we have a wonderful regulator for the soul life. A lack of conscience, the inability to listen to the warning voice of conscience, delivers us to yet other powers between the period of death and a new birth. The seer discovers souls who have become the servants of particularly evil spirit-beings after death.

Here on earth illnesses occur, and they arise in a number of different ways. We know, for instance, that in olden times epidemic sicknesses such as plague and cholera swept Europe. Materialistic science is able to point to the external causes but it cannot grasp the inner spiritual origin. Yet everything that happens has a spiritual foundation. If someone should say that science has the task to discover the physical causes of happenings, then one can always add that spiritual science does not exclude the reality of outer causes when they are justified. Spiritual science supplies the spiritual causes to the phenomena.

A person once asked the following question in connection with spiritual causes. "Can we not explain Napoleon's passionate fondness for conducting battles by the fact that when his mother carried him she would often go for walks over battle fields? Is this not a case of physical heredity?" There is something in this, but Napoleon found his way to his mother; he implanted this liking into her.

For instance, someone might say, "Here is a man. Why does he live?" The materialistic might reply, "Because he breathes." Another might respond, "But I know better.

He would not be alive today if I had not pulled him out of the water three months ago!" Yet is this last statement not correct in spite of the first? One all too readily imagines that the findings of natural science are repudiated by spiritual science. Even if it is possible to show that a person owes this or that faculty to his father and grandfather by way of heredity, it is nonetheless true that he himself has created the appropriate conditions.

Thus it is possible to study the causes of illnesses on a purely scientific basis. One can also ask the question quite externally of why has this or that person died young. But this, too, has its source in the spiritual world. In order that illnesses manifest themselves on earth, certain spiritual entities must direct them from the spiritual into the physical world.

The spiritual investigator is confronted by a shattering experience when he turns his spiritual gaze to souls who have died prematurely in the flower of youth, either as a result of illness, misfortune or hardships during their lifetimes. There are many such destinies. The seer beholds a vast expanse of illness and death wholly governed by certain evil spirit entities who bring disease and death down to the earth. If one now seeks to trace the course of existence of those souls who lacked conscience on earth, one finds that they were forced to become the servants of the evil spirits of death, disease and hindrance who bring about premature deaths and great misfortune. That is the connection.

Life only becomes comprehensible when one considers the total picture, not merely the small segment between birth and death. For this period is again closely related to what took place during the unborn condition, during the prenatal existence in the pure spiritual world. Our whole being is dependent on what occurred previously in the spirit-world. This can be understood most readily if one studies a phenomenon by means of supersensible cognition that might appear to many as an objection to spiritual investigation as such.

There are people who say, "You seek to trace faculties and destinies of human beings to previous earth lives, but consider the Bernoulli family in whom there were eight mathematicians! Surely that shows clearly that certain faculties are passed from generation to generation by way of heredity."

If, however, such a phenomenon is carefully studied by means of supersensible cognition, the following result is reached. Everything that manifests itself on earth in this or that artistic form, that permeates the human being with a sense for the spiritual—and art always does this—has its origin in the supersensible world. A person who brings artistic gifts into the world does so because of previous earth lives, or by virtue of a special act of grace during the period before birth, before conception, when he lived in a special manner in the realm of the harmony of the spheres. Now he manifests a certain affinity towards that physical body able to provide the faculty he has perceived and thus bring it to expression in earthly life.

No soul would seek to incarnate in a body in such a family where musical gifts are in the hereditary stream unless he had acquired in a previous earth life the very faculties needed for that art, unless he had passed through the period between death and rebirth in order to be reborn in a musical body. For only the most primitive predispositions can be found in the hereditary stream. A good musical ear is inherited. The organs are transformed according to the particular faculties of the soul during the embryonic period or after birth. The first instrument on which man plays is his own organism, and this is truly a most complex instrument. Divine spiritual beings have needed the whole of the Saturn, Sun and Moon periods of evolution in order to fashion this instrument. We come into the world with a wisdom that far exceeds what we are able to acquire later.

Man imagines that he has reached a considerable degree of wisdom when he begins to be able to think. But the wisdom we develop when we begin to think is in fact far smaller in comparison to the great wisdom that we acquired but lost at a particular time. At birth our brain is still soft. The connecting links that go from the brain to the several organs are still undeveloped, and we are endowed with wisdom during childhood in order to "plan-in" the organs, the instrument.

The moment to which we look back as the first occasion on which we were conscious of ourselves marks the time when we lost the faculty to play on our instrument. This ability is much greater in early childhood than later on. A profound wisdom is utilized in order to bring us to the point at which we become this intricate instrument. This fact can permeate us with a deep sense of admiration for what we are as long as we rest within the womb of divine spiritual wisdom. Then we become aware that we actually come into life with a much greater wisdom than is normally realized. Then we can also picture the vastness of the wisdom that surrounds us in our existence that precedes the embryonic stage. This is of the utmost significance, for initiate consciousness perceives that the farther back we go the greater is the wisdom and ability of man.

Now let us consider with supersensible perception the soul of an individual who has become the servant of an evil spirit of disease and death. Such a soul enables us to see how the wisdom of which man is capable has been extinguished, how he has lowered himself. Such a soul offers a terrifying aspect. Once destined to develop the loftiest wisdom, he is now so degraded that he has become the servant of ahrimanic beings! Man has the alternative during an incarnation when he has surrounded himself with a physical body either to receive the spiritual world into himself, to participate in spiritual life, to animate his soul so that after death he experiences the spiritual world around him, or to dull himself. Such souls have dulled themselves because they failed to receive between birth and death what would have enabled them to perceive a spiritual world around them.

Thus we see how individual souls are connected with the spiritual life of the world as a whole. Thus we see ourselves membered in the totality of life on earth. So also we understand the importance of not letting our innate spirit-powers wither, but of cultivating them lest we gradually be obliterated from the world. A person could maintain, however, that he wants to obliterate himself from the surrounding world because to him life is meaningless. To extinguish oneself in this way is not destruction. It merely represents an extinguishing of oneself in relation to the surrounding world. Although one is then no longer there for the surrounding world, one is nevertheless there for oneself. To extinguish oneself in the world means to be condemned to loneliness in the spiritual world. It is as if one lived in utter solitude, cut off, robbed of any means of communication.

This is what one achieves if one excludes oneself from the spiritual world.

You may well make use of the following picture. Let it impress itself upon you for it can be considered as a sound basis for meditation.

The more a person advances in the evolution of the world, the freer he becomes. He will live more and more as if on an island and his calls, his understanding must go from island to island. Human beings who seek to partake of the future of the spiritual life of humanity will be able to understand one another, that is, those who live in freedom on other islands. Those, on the other hand, who flee the spiritual life will find themselves on their own individual islands, and when they seek to communicate with those whom they knew previously, they will be unable to do so. The voice that calls will be stifled in them. Each will sense, "Over there on those islands are those whom I know, with whom I am connected." But nothing will penetrate to him and he will listen but hear nothing.

Spiritual science provides the language that in the future will enable men to gain the possibility to bridge the gap of loneliness and reach an understanding. The utterances that come to us out of occult writings are often more profound than we imagine. When the Mystery of Golgotha took place, humanity received the first proclamation that man needs in order to reach an understanding from one island to the other.

The second proclamation is by way of anthroposophical spiritual science, which seeks to clarify ever more the Christ mystery for the soul of man. The actual words of Christ are indicated in many of his sayings. Among the most profound of them all is, "When two are gathered in my name, I will be among them." One will learn to understand this Name only when one masters the language of the spirit.

In the early phase of the Christian proclamation one still found it in a naïve manner. In the future only those human souls will know the Christ who recognize Him by way of spiritual science.

To many people it may appear ridiculous that spiritual science is termed the spiritual language that humanity needs so that people will not be isolated after death, but will find the possibility of traveling from one island to the other.

The subject with which we have dealt today will give you the reason why we gather in order to cultivate spiritual science. He who works consciously for spiritual science follows that call, that voice. He also follows it who merely feels a longing to hear something about the spiritual world. These voices, these calls come from the spiritual world, and so does the need that is experienced in the spiritual world when those who dwell between death and a new birth are heard. And the voices of the various hierarchical beings can also be heard.

These voices as they sound forth towards us will awaken in our souls what will lead humanity to cultivate increasingly the spiritual life that is also nurtured in our groups. May it also continue to be cultivated faithfully here.

That is the wish that I would like to express to you at the end of these considerations, and it is my deepest hope that it may grow ever stronger, kindling your souls so that the work of spiritual science may take fire and be carried forward out of true anthroposophical warmth.

ANTHROPOSOPHY AS THE QUICKENER

OF FEELING AND OF LIFE

Tübingen, February 16, 1913

X

ANTHROPOSOPHY AS THE QUICKENER
OF FEELING AND OF LIFE

Tübingen, February 16, 1913

IF WE pause in our anthroposophical considerations and raise the question of what attracts us to such a spiritual movement as our own, then naturally we can provide an answer from a variety of aspects. One of the most important aspects that engages our feelings most deeply, though not the only one, is the consideration of the life of the human soul between death and a new birth. In fact, the happenings that occur during the long period between death and rebirth are truly not less significant than the events between birth and death. We can consider now only a few of the most important events that we experience. But one may add that in such considerations one has the profound conviction that humanity is approaching a period when it must know and experience something of supersensible worlds.

Let us broach the matter concretely. When the seer who is able to perceive life between death and rebirth meets the following event, this in itself is sufficient for him to feel it a duty to work towards a cognition of the spiritual world. A person has died. The seer seeks to find him some time after he has passed through the gate of death. In the manner that one can communicate with the dead one may gather the following from him. I am quoting an actual instance, "I have left my wife behind on the earth; I know that she is still there." Obviously this is not conveyed by means of earthly words. "When I was living with her in the physical world she was always like sunshine to me as I came home from work. I experienced her words like a blessing and I could not have conceived of life without the light-filled presence of my beloved companion. Then I went through the gate of death and left her behind, and now I long to go back. I feel the lack of all I had. Longingly in my soul I seek a path to my life-long companion but I cannot find her. I cannot penetrate into her presence. It is as if she were not there. When from time to time I feel as if she were there, as if I were with her, then she appears unable to speak. It can be compared to two people, one of whom would like the other to say a few words, but the other is dumb and unable to say anything. And so the soul who was a blessing to me during the long span of physical existence has become dumb."

Now if one investigates the basis of such facts one finds the following answer. In this case there is simply no common language between the one who has died and the one who remains on earth. There is nothing that could permeate the soul with that substance by means of which it would remain perceptible. Because there is no common language, these two souls feel severed from one another. This was not always so.

If we go back in the evolution of mankind, we find that souls possessed a spiritual inheritance that enabled them to remain perceptible, irrespective of whether they were both on the physical plane or one in the physical and the other in the spiritual world. That spiritual inheritance is exhausted today. It is no longer present, and the painful case just described occurs where the soul of a loved one cannot be found after death because in the soul of the one who has remained on earth there is nothing that can render it perceptible to the one who has died. What can in fact be seen by the dead is spiritual knowledge, feeling and experience. That is the connection of souls here on earth with the spiritual world. If a soul who has been left behind on earth occupies himself with knowledge of the spiritual worlds, allows such thoughts to cross his mind, then these thoughts can be perceived by the one who has died. The religious feelings of the past are no longer sufficient to give the soul what it needs in order to be perceived by the dead.

If he pursues the matter further, the seer discovers that even when these souls have gone through the gate of death, they have but a dim perception of one another. They will only be able to achieve a mutual understanding under considerable difficulty, or not at all, because a common language is lacking.

The seer realizes what anthroposophy is in a deeper sense. It is the language that will be spoken by the living and the dead, by those who live in the physical world and those who dwell between death and rebirth.

Souls who remain behind and have acquired thoughts about the supersensible worlds can be seen by the dead. If they have radiated love before death, they can also do so after death. This carries the conviction that anthroposophy is a language that renders it possible for those in supersensible realms to perceive the events of the physical world.

The prospect that stands before humanity is that souls will become even more lonely, will be unable to find a bridge to one another, unless a link is forged from soul to soul by means of spiritual concepts. That is the reality of anthroposophy, for it is not a theory.

Theoretical knowledge is of the least importance. What we take into ourselves is a genuine soul elixir, a real substance. This substance enables the soul who has gone through the gate of death to perceive the soul who has remained behind. In fact, the seer who has gained insight into such a situation, where the one who has died cannot find those he has left behind because that family has not connected itself with spiritual science, knows that he can follow no other course than to speak to his fellow men about spiritual wisdom. He sees the sorrow with which the soul is burdened by such a lack of communication. He knows that the time has come when spiritual wisdom must take hold of human hearts.

Those whose mission to speak about the supersensible stems from the knowledge of the spiritual worlds, experience it as an urgent necessity that they cannot counter in any way. It would be the greatest sin if they did so. They feel it a necessity to proclaim revelations about the supersensible worlds.

From what has just been said you can gather the immense seriousness connected with the proclamation of spiritual revelation. There is, however, yet another aspect to the understanding between the living and the dead. In this connection we have not progressed very far as yet but it will come about. In order to grasp how the living will gradually develop an understanding for the dead, let us consider the following.

Man knows little about the physical world. How does he gain knowledge of this world? He makes use of his senses, brings his imagination to bear, has certain sensations conveyed to him by the external world. But that is only the minutest portion of the content of the world. There is something quite other contained in it.

I would like you to realize that there is something of far greater importance than sense reality. I do not mean the supersensible world, but something other than that.

Imagine for a moment that you are in the habit of leaving home every morning at eight in order to go to work. One day you suddenly notice you are leaving three minutes later. You go through a particular place where there is a kind of overhang, the roof of which is supported by pillars. When you arrive there three minutes later than usual you realize that if you had arrived on time, you would have been crushed by the falling roof. Imagine this quite vividly! It does happen that a person misses a train that is later involved in an accident. Had he caught the train he would have been killed. When such things do not occur we pay no attention to them. If you become dramatically aware of such an occurrence, it makes a certain impression on you. Similar things, which fail to strike you in the course of the day, can happen from morning till night. They cannot be surveyed. Such occurrences may appear as "clever conjecture," and yet they belong to the most important aspects of life.

To take another example, you gain a particular feeling when you consider that a man in Berlin had already got his ticket for the *Titanic*. He meets a friend who urges him not to sail on the *Titanic*. The friend succeeds in persuading him not to sail on this ship. The *Titanic* sinks, and he escapes from death. This makes a lasting impression on the person concerned!

That is a special case, and yet such things are happen-

187

ing all the time without being noticed. When one does become aware of them they make an impression on the heart and mind.

Let us consider this matter from another aspect. How many impressions of heart and mind escape us because we have been protected unawares from danger! If we were aware of the many things from which we are constantly preserved, we would go about the world in a totally different frame of mind. Furthermore, the seer discovers the following possibility. Let us assume that things actually happened in the way described. You arrived three minutes later than usual at that spot. This is the most opportune moment for a person who has died to make himself perceptible to your soul. You may have the feeling, "Where does that come from that arises in my soul?" It need not occur only in such a special case as quoted. It may take manifold forms. A beginning will be made when people become attentive not only to the world of outer reality but also to the sphere of probabilities. The considerable number of herring in the ocean is a reality. They become possible only because a vast quantity of eggs was released. In this way an infinite number of possibilities forms the basis of life.

This makes a profound impression on the seer also when he reaches the boundary of two worlds. He feels, "How infinitely rich in possibilities is the spiritual world. Only a minute part of it becomes reality in our sense world!" This is accompanied by the feeling, "An enormous amount lies hidden in the very ground of being." This feeling grows as one occupies oneself with anthroposophy. One develops the feeling that at every point where something happens externally a hidden something lies behind it. Each flower, each breath of air, each stone and crystal hides an endless number of possibilities. Ultimately this feeling will bring about a growing sense of devotion towards what is hidden. As this feeling develops, one will quite naturally become aware that at such moments they can communicate with one who for earthly life is dead. In the future it will occur quite normally that a person will feel that the dead has spoken to his soul. Gradually he will realize from whom the communication comes, that is, who has spoken into him. It is only because people are so little aware of the endless, fathomless realm of possibilities that they cannot hear what the dead would speak to the hearts of the living

This twofold consideration will indicate the radical change that will be brought about for the whole of humanity by the spreading of anthroposophy. On the one hand, the thoughts of anthroposophists will become perceptible for the dead. On the other, the dead will be able to speak to the hearts of those who have developed a spiritual sensitivity. A bridge will be built between this world and the world beyond. In fact, life between death and rebirth will also be different. This will not be mere theory, but reality. An understanding will be achieved between the so-called living and the dead, who are in fact far more alive. Souls on earth will also feel what is fruitful for the dead. One cannot really make life fruitful for them unless one feels what an immense service one bestows on the dead by reading to them.

Let us consider an extreme case. One will no doubt have come across it in relation to other people. One lives with a sister, parents, a husband or a wife. The more the one feels the urge to connect himself closely to anthroposophy, the more the other develops a strong animosity towards it. How

189

often can one experience this! It may take this form in consciousness, but it need not be so in the soul itself. There something different may take place.

The unconscious works in the astral body. It may be that the more a person slanders and rages against spiritual science, the more deeply in his unconsciousness he harbors an urge, a longing, to hear about spiritual science.

When we go through the gate of death we encounter truth. There nothing can be concealed. Here on earth one can lie and pretend but after death things take on their true coloring. Things reveal themselves as they really are.

However much one has stupefied oneself and slandered spiritual science during one's lifetime, after death an urge towards it is noticeable. One suffers because this urge cannot be satisfied. But now the living can imagine himself in the presence of the dead, and he can think spiritual thoughts and the dead will understand. Even if the one who died was not an anthroposophist, the dead will nevertheless be able to perceive the living one who occupies himself with spiritual thoughts.

There is a certain inclination on the part of the dead towards the language he used to speak during his lifetime, because during the early phases after death he is still connected with his particular language. It is therefore advisable to clothe one's thoughts in the language the dead used to speak. But after five, six, eight years, and on occasion earlier, we find that the language of the spirit is such that the external language presents no obstacle whatever. The one who died can also understand spiritual thoughts in a language that he did not know during his lifetime.

At any rate, the outcome of reading to the dead, even if

they were not anthroposophists, has proved itself to be particularly beautiful. It has shown itself to be a special service and one of the greatest deeds of love that can be performed.

In order to reach our aims it is not only a question of spreading anthroposophy externally—this must be done and it is important—but anthroposophy must also be cultivated more quietly within the recesses of the soul. Spiritual positions of responsibility may be created by means of which much can be achieved for the development of the soul after death. It must be our aim to help to overcome obstacles for souls who live between death and rebirth, because the old spiritual inheritance has been exhausted, and the time has come when souls find it exceedingly difficult to orient themselves after death. Some find it almost impossible to do so.

The seer also sees souls between death and rebirth who are compelled to carry out tasks that they themselves do not understand. For example, the seer may discover souls in that realm who are the servants of the powers of death and disease for a period of time. This does not refer to the regular occurrence of death but to events relating to people being taken away in the flower of youth. Illnesses are of a physical nature. They are caused, however, by powers that play in from supersensible realms. Epidemic illnesses can be traced back to the deeds of supersensible beings and certain spirits have the task of bringing about untimely death. We cannot discuss now how this can be substantiated as part of a wise guidance, but it is important to note that certain souls are yoked to such beings. Although the seer must have accustomed himself to a certain equanimity, such situations are painful and shattering to behold. Such souls are compelled to serve and bring death and disease to mankind.

If the seer looks back into the lives of such souls before death, he discovers why they are condemned to serve as servants to the spirits of death and disease. The cause lies in a lack of conscience in such souls during their earthly life. In accordance with the extent of their lack of conscience they condemn themselves to become servants of those evil beings. As truly as cause and effect obtain in the case of impinging billiard balls, so, too, must people who have no conscience become servants of these evil beings. That is indeed shattering!

The seer beholds yet another fact. Souls who are under the yoke of ahrimanic beings have to prepare the spiritual origin of all that occurs on earth as obstacles, as impediments to our deeds. Ahriman also has this task. All obstacles that arise here on earth are directed from the spiritual world. They are servants of Ahriman. Why have such souls condemned themselves to such service? Because during their lives on earth they indulged in love of ease and comfort. If you but consider how widespread love of ease has become, you will find that Ahriman has a considerable number of recruits. Love of ease is uppermost in life today. Modern economists do not only reckon with egoism and competition, but also with the comfort of the human being. Love of ease and comfort are important factors.

Now there is a difference in whether one has such experiences and is able to understand why one has them or whether one experiences them quite unconsciously without realizing why one has to serve such spirits. If one knows why one is yoked to the spirits that bring epidemics about, one also realizes the virtues that have to be developed in the next life in order to work towards a cosmic compensation. If one remains ignorant of the reason, one does in fact create the same karma, but the compensation can only occur in a second incarnation. Actual progress is thereby postponed.

It is important, therefore, that man should learn about such things on earth. One will experience them after death but one learns to orient oneself down here. Here we have yet another fact that makes it essential to bring about a new sense of orientation by spreading spiritual truths. The old means of orientation are no longer available.

We can ask, "Why are we anthroposophists?" We can give an answer out of the spiritual facts themselves that speaks directly to our feelings rather than to our intellect. So anthroposophy becomes increasingly a universal language. It becomes a language that will render it possible to tear down the partition that stands between the different worlds in which we live, one time in a physical body, another without a physical body. Thus the wall between the physical and the spiritual world will crumble when spiritual science really takes hold of the souls of men. We should feel this. It can give us the right inner enthusiasm for spiritual science.

Let me bring another matter to your attention. For the seer there is during the lives of souls between death and rebirth a moment that reveals itself of special importance. It is also of importance for others after death. For some this point lies earlier, for others, later. If one beholds the life of sleep with supersensible cognition, one sees the human being with his astral body and ego outside the physical body. Looking back, one gains the impression that the physical body is slowly dying.

It is only from the first years of infancy until the child develops an understanding, until the moment that memory begins, that the body during sleep has a blooming, flourishing appearance. A slow withering process in the physical body sets in shortly after life begins. Death is but the final occurrence in this dying process. Sleep is there in order to compensate for the forces that have been exhausted but the compensation is incomplete. Each time there remains a small residue of death forces. When so much residue has been accumulated that the upbuilding forces are unequal to the task, physical death ensues. Therefore, as one considers the human physical body one sees how death gradually fulfills itself. In reality we slowly die from birth onwards. This makes a solemn impression as one becomes aware of the facts.

Between death and rebirth the moment occurs when forces begin to develop in the soul that lead to a next incarnation. Let me attempt to explain what I mean by way of an example. There are a number of books that deal with Goethe's predisposition. One examines Goethe's ancestors in order to ascertain the hereditary origin of this or that quality. The sources are sought within the physical hereditary line of descent. I have no quarrel with the fact that they can be found there, but he who can trace the life of soul between death and rebirth discovers the following.

Let us take the soul of Goethe. For a long time before birth the soul worked on its ancestors out of the supersensible worlds, and because of its own forces, developed a relationship with its forefathers. The soul even worked to the extent of bringing together those men and women who could provide over a long period of time the appropriate predispositions needed by that individuality. This is not an easy task because many souls are involved in this process. Picture to yourselves that from souls of the sixteenth through the eighteenth centuries human beings descend. All these souls must already have collaborated, and you will gather from this that such a working together is a matter of great importance. Souls born in the eighteenth and nineteenth centuries must already have reached a reciprocal understanding in the sixteenth century in order that the complete network of relationships may come about.

There is much to do between death and rebirth. Not only the objective tasks have to be performed such as the temporary service that has to be given to the spirits of opposition, but we must labor at the forces that in fact enable us to reincarnate. That means that we have to shape the general form archetypally. This makes the opposite impression from what the seer beholds when he observes the sleeping physical and etheric bodies. The physical and etheric bodies in sleep have a withering appearance, but the upbuilding of the archetype and its descent into the physical realm makes a blossoming, flourishing impression.

The important moment between death and rebirth lies at the point between the recollection of the earlier existence and the transition period where man begins to prepare so that his physical organism may come into being. If you now picture to yourselves physical death and compare it with this moment, then you have the opposite pole of physical death. Physical death marks a transition from being into non-being. The moment described above is the transition from non-being into a state of becoming. This moment is experienced quite differently if one understands it than if one does not.

The concept of the polar opposite of death, the moment that arises between death and a new birth, should become feeling within the soul of an anthroposophist. It should not merely be understood intellectually, but should become inner experience. Then we shall be able to sense how much our life is enriched when such thoughts are received by the soul.

There is yet another aspect, namely, that gradually the soul develops a feeling for all that is in the world. If, after having meditated upon the concepts I have just mentioned, one goes for a walk through a forest in the spring, one will find that one is not far removed, providing one is attentive, from experiencing the spiritual beings that weave among the physical phenomena. To experience the spiritual world in reality would not be at all difficult if human beings were not to create their own obstacles. One should attempt to translate what has been received in the form of concepts into a feeling experience, to awaken it vividly within oneself. Such a striving can lead to a beholding of the spirit. The questions I have broached today are intended as a contribution to enliven the impulse toward spiritual science. Whenever one speaks about matters such as these, one feels that it is a mere stammering because our language belongs to the physical world. One has to make a considerable effort, by way of special descriptive means, to evoke at least a limited concept of these matters. But to speak precisely about these matters in this way can release from our hearts what may be termed anthroposophically as potency of feeling.

Spiritual science should become for us that which quickens feeling and life. The acquisition of spiritual concepts should not become a matter of lesser concern. We should gladly pursue it. Yet we should also refrain from considering the concepts as of chief importance, but rather what anthroposophy can make of us as human beings.

THE MISSION OF EARTHLY LIFE AS A

TRANSITIONAL STAGE FOR THE BEYOND

Frankfurt, March 2, 1913

XI

THE MISSION OF EARTHLY LIFE AS A TRANSITIONAL STAGE FOR THE BEYOND

Frankfurt, March 2, 1913

TODAY there are still many people who maintain that a spirit-soul life may exist after death, but they wonder why we should concern ourselves with it now. We can simply live on earth with all that it offers and simply wait and see whether other forms of existence do come about after death!

Spiritual science shows, however, that during life between death and rebirth man encounters certain beings. Just as here he meets the many beings of the various kingdoms of nature, so after death he meets the beings of higher hierarchies and certain elemental beings. If a person goes through life without any sense of judgment, this is due to the fact that between death and rebirth he was unable to meet those beings who could have given him the appropriate forces to enable him to be morally and intellectually effective in this life. But the possibility and the ability to meet certain beings between death and rebirth depends on the last life. If during earthly life we do not occupy ourselves with thoughts relating to the supersensible, if during our life we have been completely immersed in the external sense world, if we only lived in our intellect inasmuch as it was directed to the physical world, then we make it impossible for ourselves between death and a new birth to encounter certain beings and to receive abilities from them for a subsequent life. The realm beyond remains dim and dark for us, and we are unable to find the forces of the higher hierarchies in the darkness. Man then between death and a new birth passes by those beings from whom he should receive forces for his next earthly life.

From whence comes the light by means of which we can illumine the darkness between death and rebirth? Where do we find it? Between death and rebirth no one gives us any light. The beings are there and we can only reach them providing we have kindled the light in our last earthly life by means of our interest in the spiritual world. After death we are unable to penetrate the darkness unless we have taken the light with us through the gate of death.

This shows how incorrect is the statement that we need not concern ourselves with things of a spiritual nature, but that we can afford to wait for what happens. In fact, if we wait and see, we shall only encounter darkness!

Earthly life is not merely a transitional stage. It has a mission. It is a necessity for the beyond, as indeed the beyond is for earthly existence. The lights for the life beyond must be carried upward from the earth. It may also happen that down here people remain dull to the supersensible world, that they simply miss the opportunity to develop certain faculties, that they fail to create instruments for the next incarnation.

A person who lacked a certain ability in this or that sphere during life goes through the gate of death. Now you see what a hopeless situation it all makes. If nothing were to intervene, the person would become less and less able. For if a person has deliberately dulled himself toward the spiritual world in one incarnation, he will be even less able in a following life to prepare organs for himself. If nothing else were to occur, things would take their course along an ever steeper slope of decline.

Something else, however, does intervene. A man who goes through life with deliberate dullness in one incarnation will find that Lucifer approaches him with his powers in the spiritual world after the second earthly life. If Lucifer did not approach him at this point, he would stumble through the thickest darkness. Because he has lived as described, Lucifer can approach him and can illumine the forces and beings needed for the next earthly incarnation. The result is that they are colored with luciferic light. Now following the dull existence, and after having been led by Lucifer between death and rebirth, he enters a new earth existence. He is now fully equipped with talents and abilities which prepare his organs so that everywhere he is open to luciferic temptations on earth.

Now such a person may be clever, but his cleverness will be cold and calculating; above all it will be permeated by selfishness, by egoism. This manifests itself to the seer in many instances where people are clever but actually cold and selfish in their activity. When one meets them they are always seeking their own advantage and do all they can to place themselves in the limelight. A consideration of such people shows that in the spiritual world they were led by Lucifer. In the previous incarnation they led a dull existence that was followed by a stumbling in the darkness after death, and this was preceded by yet another life on earth during which they deliberately closed themselves to the spiritual world.

Such an insight reveals a sad prospect for materialists. Our contemporaries who are materialistically inclined and reject all concern for the spiritual world and consider the soul life as ending with death, can expect an existence as just described. It is of little consequence to gather abstractly certain thoughts about the interrelations of various earth lives. An exact, concrete survey reveals the most manifold connections between former and later earth lives and the life in the spirit that follows each incarnation. We should hold onto the fact that life on earth is of considerable importance for life after death.

Life on earth has yet another significance. It is only on the earth that we can meet certain beings, and man belongs above all among them. Unless the link is established between man and man on earth, it cannot occur in the spirit world. The relationships between human beings are forged here and continue in the spiritual world. If we miss the opportunity to meet certain individuals on earth who were predestined to be in incarnation, we cannot make up for it during the period between death and rebirth.

Let us take the example of Gautama Buddha. He was that human personality who lived during the sixth century B.C. as the son of a king, and who rose in his twenty-ninth year from the rank of bodhisattva to that of buddha. This means that he became a buddha and no longer needed to incarnate in physical human form. The Gautama Buddha thus accomplished his last earthly life. A considerable number of people met this individuality on earth during that time, and also in earlier incarnations people had been in contact with the Bodhisattva. All these connections could be continued later in the spiritual world. The connection to Gautama Buddha, which bore the character of a pupil to teacher relationship, could be continued in the spiritual world. But there were souls who during the evolution of humanity never made a connection with Gautama Buddha on earth. These souls, even if they now have reached a considerable degree of development, cannot at all easily come in contact in the spiritual world with the being of Buddha, with the soul of the one who was incarnated as Gautama Buddha. For Gautama Buddha what may be called a replacement appears; he has a replacement if one has been unable to make a connection with him on earth.

The Buddha has had a special destiny since he rose to buddhahood and no longer needed to return to the earth thus continuing to dwell in a pure spiritual region. He remained in touch with earthly happenings, however, and worked from the spiritual worlds down into the earthly sphere. We know that the being of Gautama Buddha radiated into the Jesus child spoken of in the Gospel of St. Luke. The supersensible being of Buddha streamed into the astral body of the Luke Jesus child. It worked from the supersensible down into earthly realms. Human beings on earth could no longer find access to him. Only those could make a contact with the being of Gautama who, like Francis of Assisi, for instance, had gone through a higher form of development. Before he entered life on earth, and previous also to the last life between birth and death, the being of Francis of Assisi lived in a mystery center situated in the southeast of Europe. In this center there were no physical teachers, but teachers belonging to the supersensible hierarchy of whom Buddha, or more accurately, of whom the soul that had been incarnated in Buddha, was one. The pupils in such mystery centers had already developed lofty faculties for beholding the supersensible world. Such pupils are able to be taught by teachers who work only from the spiritual world. Thus Buddha taught in that mystery center, and Francis of Assisi in a former incarnation was his faithful and devoted pupil. At that time Francis of Assisi absorbed everything that later enabled him to receive the light-filled impulses of the higher hierarchies, and that then allowed him to appear in incarnation as the great mystic who was to exert such a strong influence on his age. This was all due to the fact that the soul of Francis of Assisi, through the higher faculties he possessed at the time, was able to establish a connection with the Gautama Buddha after the Buddha was able to work down from the supersensible world upon him.

For ordinary human beings who are dependent on life as it unfolds through the senses and the intellect, such a meeting is not possible. In that case what has been said earlier applies. We cannot meet a person in the spiritual world unless we have first met him on earth.

The exception that we have just considered in relation to the Buddha brings forth yet another. Although it is impossible for ordinary individuals to meet others in spiritual realms with whom they have not had a previous connection on earth, yet if a person has received the Christ impulse and permeates himself with it, he can nevertheless meet the Buddha after death. For the position of this being is a special one.

At the beginning of the seventeenth century another planet was involved in a crisis of development similar to that of the earth when the Mystery of Golgotha occurred.

As the Christ appeared on earth from higher realms at the time of Golgotha, so Buddha appeared on Mars during the Mars crisis of the seventeenth century. After Buddha had completed his incarnations it was no longer necessary for him to return to the earth, but he continued his activities in other realms. The Buddha wandered away from earthly affairs to the realm of Mars. Until then Mars had been the chosen center of forces designated by the Greeks as fearfully warlike. This mission of Mars came to an end in the seventeenth century. Another impulse became necessary and the Buddha accomplished a Buddha crucifixion there. The Buddha Mystery on Mars did not take the same course as the Christ Mystery on earth, but Buddha, the Prince of Peace, who, during his last earthly life had spread peace and love wherever he went, was transferred to the belligerent realm of Mars. The fact that a being who is fully permeated by forces of peace and love was transferred to a realm of strife and disharmony may in a sense be regarded as a crucifixion. For the seer two happenings come together in a most wonderful way. One beholds, on the one hand, the eighty-year-old dying Buddha, and this death has a deeply moving, deeply stirring quality. Buddha died in 483 surrounded by silver rays on a wonderful moonlit night, radiating peace and compassion. That was his last earthly hour. And then he was active again in the way described. The seer discovers him kindling the compassionate, silvery, moral light of Buddha on Mars at the beginning of the seventeenth century. These two wonderful events are deeply related in the course of world history.

The human souls who have received the Christ impulse into themselves in the corresponding manner here on earth travel through the cosmic universe after death. We all go through these cosmic realms. To begin with, we go through the planets of our planetary system. We experience a Moon period, a Mercury period, a Venus period, a Sun period, a Mars period, a Jupiter period and a Saturn period. Following these we go into the surroundings of our planetary system and then later commence our return journey. Now we encounter those forces and the beings from whom we must receive what we need to build up our next earthly life. He who has received the Christ impulse on earth can also receive what streams from the Buddha in his passage through the Mars sphere. This belongs to the exceptional case in which souls who have not been together with Buddha in earlier incarnations nevertheless have the opportunity of meeting him between death and rebirth.

Supersensible perception reveals that a number of personalities who lived during the seventeenth century owed their remarkable talents to the fact that during their prenatal life in the spiritual world they received an impulse from Buddha. At present the ability to receive such talents is still limited among human beings because it is only comparatively recently that the Buddha accomplished the Mystery on Mars. In future, human souls will be more and more capable of receiving the Buddha impulse from the Mars sphere. But in the nineteenth century there were already some personalities—and this was disclosed to those able to perceive it—who were able to develop their faculties here on earth as a result of the influences they received from Buddha through their passage in the Mars sphere. The course of life between death and rebirth is indeed complex and wonderful.

Unless man is able to take with him the light to illumine his experience between death and rebirth, he stumbles in the dark. This also holds good for this exceptional case. A person who departs from the earth through the gate of death without having taken the Christ impulse into himself, who wished to know nothing of it, will not have the slightest intimation of the influences of Buddha during his next life in the spiritual world as he passes through the Mars sphere. For him it is as if the Buddha were not present. It should be borne in mind that we encounter the beings of the Higher Hierarchies, but whether or not we perceive them and establish the right connection with them depends on whether we kindled a light in our last earthly existence so that we do not pass them by and are able to receive impulses from them. That is why it is a complete fallacy to maintain that it is unnecessary to concern oneself with the beyond during earthly existence.

You will gather from the foregoing that from a higher aspect life on earth really constitutes a special case. We live embodied within a special organism on earth between life and death. Apart from an earthly incarnation one can speak of an "embodiment" between death and rebirth, or rather of an "ensouling." What I have elaborated in connection with the spiritual world also applies to the earth. Consider that a human being living between death and rebirth may pass through the Mars sphere without entering it in the slightest connection with the beings who inhabit Mars. He does not see them, and they are not aware of him. This is true of the earth also. Beings belonging to other planets, just as man belongs to the earth, are continually passing through the earth sphere. The inhabitants of Mars spend the normal course of their life on Mars, and during their experience, which corresponds on Mars to the period between death and a new life but yet is different, they pass through the planetary spheres. So that in fact inhabitants of other planets are continually passing through our earth sphere. Human beings are unable to establish any contact with them because they live under quite different conditions and because they will in the main not have made the least connection with these beings on Mars.

What would be the conditions necessary in order to meet the beings from other planets as they pass through the earth sphere? One would have had to develop points of contact with them in their own planetary realms, but this is only possible if on earth one has already reached the stage of being able to contact beings other than those of the earth as a result of the development of supersensible powers.

Thus the possibility is there for those who have undergone a higher development to encounter the beings who wander through from other planets. It may sound peculiar and yet it is so, that for those who have intercourse with the wanderers from Mars and learn to know of the nature of that planet, the strange theories that physics and astronomy weave about Mars inhabitants appear most comical, for the facts are quite different.

I bring forth these things so that you can widen your gaze from earthly existence into other realms extending beyond the visible beings that surround us to beings who cannot be perceived unless we develop the organs to behold them. But between death and rebirth we also cannot establish a connection with conditions belonging to the mission of the earth unless we have first contacted them by way of the earth.

What is spiritual science or anthroposophy from a cosmic aspect? He who weaves theories might easily believe that spiritual science is something that can be taught and learned in all realms of the cosmos, but that is not the same. Each realm has its own particular task and it does not repeat itself in other realms. Spiritual science is only possible on earth, not on other planets or in other realms. The creative powers have so made the earth that only here can certain things arise. Spiritual science can only arise on earth. Nowhere else can it be learned. It is a revelation of the supersensible world but in such a form as can arise only here on earth.

One might well say that supposing all this to be true, surely one could be instructed about the supersensible in the spiritual world in a form other than that of spiritual science! One can certainly think this, but it is not true. For if a person is at all predisposed to gain a genuine connection with higher worlds, he can do so only by means of spiritual science. If he fails to draw near to spiritual science or anthroposophy on earth, no other form of existence will help him to get to know it. But no other form of existence will help him to gain a genuine human connection with the supersensible worlds, either.

This need not plunge us into despair about the many people who are still refusing to know anything about anthroposophy. They will return and establish a connection with it at a later stage. Anthroposophy has been established on the earth in such a way as to impart to people what has to be known about the supersensible worlds in accordance with the nature of man. Only one form of communication is possible and that is by way of human beings. If a person goes through the gate of death without having heard anything of spiritual science on earth, he can become familiar with it through the fact that he knew a person who had a connection with spiritual science. This is a round-about path but a possible one.

Let us take the example of two people who were on friendly terms during their earthly life. One has made a connection with anthroposophy, the other not. The latter dies. The former can help him considerably by reading to him, by making him familiar with what surrounds him after death. A person can read an important work of spiritual science with the dead and, as the seer will confirm, the dead listens attentively.

It is also a fact that a simple person who has only just come in touch with spiritual science may be better able to read to a deceased person whom he genuinely loved than the seer who, though able to find the soul of the dead, had no affectionate connection with him in this life. From time to time it may also happen that seers give themselves the task of reading to the souls of the dead whom they have not known. Yet more often than not one is unable to read to a dead person with whom one has had no previous connection on earth.

These facts will impress upon you the importance of spiritual communities such as the anthroposophical one because here we find to a certain extent a replacement for what may be called a kind of living together and getting in touch.

Should such communities not exist, each soul after death would have to rely entirely on being read to by people close to them. Only such spiritual communities where spiritual ideals are commonly fostered can expand this sphere. Thus it can and does happen that one meets an anthroposophist who, because of what he has previously learned, is able in a special way, to read a spiritual content with much concentration or to let such thoughts pass through his soul. One might approach him, mention to him that a person who dies was also an anthroposophist, belonged to the same society, and show him a sample of the writing of the deceased. It may suffice that by seeing the writing or by hearing a favorite verse of the deceased, the more developed anthroposophist is able to read to such a soul in a most fruitful manner, though he did not know him on earth. It is indeed a fine task for a spiritual community to bridge so strongly the gap between the living and the dead.

Today anthroposophists still conceive of many tasks that lie merely on the physical plane because materialistic ways of thought are still prevalent among them, though theoretically they may have absorbed the science of anthroposophy. The true spiritual tasks will present themselves when spiritual science will have penetrated the soul more deeply. People will be found to take on the task of helping the dead so that they may evolve. A beginning has been made within our movement and what already has been achieved in this sphere can give us a high degree of satisfaction.

In fact, in certain circumstances when an anthroposophist goes through the gate of death carrying spiritual thoughts with him, he may be able to serve the dead and could become their teacher. This, however, is more complicated than is usually imagined. It is easier to do this from the earth because the communities that are formed after death depend entirely on the groups that were formed before death.

If two people, for instance, lived with one another on earth, the one an anthroposophist and the other not, the one who had an aversion towards spiritual science will long for it after death. It may happen that the anthroposophist who remains behind on earth concerns himself until his death with the departed soul by reading to him. Now after a certain period of time the anthroposophist also goes through the gate of death. He is then re-united with the other in the spiritual world. An echo of the earlier connection on earth is now felt, and this presents a difficulty. There was no difficulty as long as the one was on earth and the other in the spiritual world. Dissonances arise again as they did in the earthly relationship now that they are once more united. Just as on earth the one soul did not wish to know anything about spiritual science, so it becomes again the case in the world beyond. This shows to what extent the relationships after death are dependent upon the previous earthly connections. These matters are exceedingly complex and cannot be merely thought out intellectually.

Such instances clearly reveal the mission of spiritual science. The gulf between the living and the dead must be bridged. Under certain conditions the dead can also work into the earthly sphere, as the living are able to send their influence into the spiritual world, and we can investigate how the dead work into the physical world.

As a matter of fact, people know little of what surrounds them on earth. How do they view life? The events of life as they unfold are strung on a thread, as it were. Some are considered to be causes, others effects, but beyond this little thought is given to the matter. It may sound strange that the actual things that happen form the smallest content of real life. They only represent the external content. There is yet another sphere of life apart from the things that happen, and this is of no less importance for life.

Let us take an example. A person is in the habit of leaving home punctually every morning at eight. He has a definite way to go, across a square. One day circumstances are such that he leaves three minutes later than usual. He now notices something strange on the square, under the colonnade where he used to walk every day. The roof of the colonnade has collapsed! Had he left at the accustomed time, the falling roof certainly would have killed him.

There are many such instances in life. We often find that had circumstances been different, this or that might have taken quite another course. We are protected from many dangers. Much of what could happen does not come to pass. In life we consider the external realities, not the inner possibilities. Yet these possibilities constantly lie concealed behind the actual events. The events of a particular day only constitute the external reality of life. Behind them lies an entire world of possibilities.

Take the sea as an example. In it there lives a multitude of herring but for them to arise, not only as many eggs as herring had to be present. An endless number of eggs are destroyed. Only a relatively small number of herring come to life. So is it with the whole of life. What we experience from morning until night constitutes only a portion of an enormous number of possibilities. We are continually led past certain possible events that do not actually happen. When a possible event passes us by, this marks a special moment for us. Consider the instance of the man. If he had left his house at the usual time he would have been killed by the roof of the colonnade. Such possibilities constantly accompany us in life. Such a moment, when a man would have been struck had he arrived three minutes earlier, marks an opportune occasion for the spiritual world to light up in him. He may then have an experience that can bring him together with the dead. Today people are not yet aware of such occasions because fundamentally they only live on the surface of life.

Spiritual science aims gradually to become a life elixir. Man then will not only behold external reality but he will pay attention to the stirrings in his soul life. There he will frequently find the voices of the dead who still want something from the living.

As we have an example of how the living can influence the dead by reading to them, so we also see how the dead can influence the living. A time will come when man will converse spiritually with the dead. People will speak with the dead, and they will listen to the dead. Death only marks a change in the outer form of man; his soul develops further. At present we experience as yet a most imperfect condition of mankind inasmuch as men are unable to communicate with their fellow men who dwell in another form of life. When spiritual science is no longer a theory but has permeated souls, a living communion with the dead will continually be possible. In fact, conditions, which in a sense obtain only for the seer at present, will gradually become the common heritage of the whole of humanity.

You may say, "Well, that may be so for the seer. He can find human beings between death and rebirth." Actually, this presents considerable difficulties today because the general lack of belief in the spiritual world, the lack of connection to the spirit, creates hindrances also for those who could establish a relationship to the spiritual world.

There are certain things that can take place unhindered only if they belong to the common possession of humanity. A man may be an outstandingly gifted master-builder. If nobody engages his services, he will not be able to build. This also can be the case for the seer. He may possess the faculties to ascend spiritually to the realm of the dead but if this process is hindered owing to the fact that communion with the dead is impossible for most people, the seer will only be able to succeed in establishing a contact in a few exceptional instances.

My dear friends, I wished to show you how spiritual science can be a life-giving impulse. More than anything we may learn theoretically, it is important to cultivate a feeling for the task of spiritual science in relation to the future of humanity. This enables each one who belongs to the anthroposophical movement to gain an impression of what he is really doing. He gains an impression of the tremendous task that has to be achieved by spiritual science or anthroposophy. This also enables one to connect oneself earnestly and worthily to spiritual science, not in a light-hearted way, as to something that is to refresh one but as an impulse which will become of ever increasing importance as mankind advances into the future. I wished to evoke a feeling for this by today's considerations.

LIFE BETWEEN DEATH AND REBIRTH

Munich, March 10-12, 1913

XII

LIFE BETWEEN DEATH AND REBIRTH

The Connection between the Physical
and the Supersensible World

Munich, March 10, 1913

In MATERIALISTIC circles a phrase is currently in use
which, though quite sensible from an outer aspect, acquires
a totally different complexion when viewed in the light of
spiritual science. It was prevalent at the time when theoretical materialism flourished and gained widespread popu-
larity. Yet, even today this phrase is still used: Assuming
that there is a life after death we need not concern ourselves
with it until we get there because when we cross the gate
of death we shall see what happens. As for our physical existence, it is sufficient to plunge into it, and one may hope,
if indeed there is a life beyond, that one is thereby adequately prepared to enter it.

In the light of supersensible cognition capable of beholding the realm that man crosses between death and rebirth,
such a way of speaking is pure nonsense. When we cross the
gate of death we are, to begin with, occupied with the remains, the memories and the connections of our last earthly
embodiment. For a period of decades during the first stages
after death, an individual looks back in retrospect in a
sense on his last incarnation. He is still involved with what

remains in the astral body as forces from the last earthly life but increasingly he enters into the sphere that we described from a cosmic aspect on a previous occasion. He gradually enters a realm where he comes into contact with the beings of the higher hierarchies. Man must encounter these beings because this enables him to gather the forces he needs when later on, through birth, he again enters physical existence.

The human being has to bring with him two things that have been elaborated and strengthened between death and rebirth. He has to bring with him the forces which, once he has connected himself with the stream of heredity, enable him to fashion plastically his corporeal form from within outwards for many years to come, in order that the bodily constitution may be fully adapted to the individuality that he has brought over from previous earth lives. What is provided by way of our ancestors in the physical hereditary stream only corresponds to the individuality inasmuch as we are attracted by the mixture within the hereditary stream, so to speak, that arises because of the nature of our forefathers. Man is attracted by the potentialities within the physical hereditary stream, but what he receives as his outer sheath by going through birth, first has to be fashioned in its finer aspects. This is made possible by means of a remarkably complex structure of forces that he brings with him from the spiritual world and receives in such a form that one particular hierarchical order bestows these, another those, forces. To express it in a pictorial way we could say, man between death and rebirth receives those gifts from the beings of the higher hierarchies that he needs in order to adapt to his individuality what is obtained by means of heredity.

This is the one aspect we have to consider in the incarnating human being. The other is that even if he remains unaware of it, he has to work at the elaboration and formation of his destiny. Much of what appears as chance occurrence in life is actually conditioned by means of the forces he has acquired between death and rebirth that enable him to bring about precisely what lies in his karma. This indicates how man receives the gifts of the beings of the hierarchies whom he encounters between death and a new birth.

Supersensible perception confirms that the human soul can journey through the realm between death and a new birth in a twofold way. It is possible for the soul to wander through the realm of the higher hierarchies as if stumbling in the darkness without being able to receive the corresponding gifts from the higher hierarchies because of inner tendencies. In order to receive the gifts from the higher hierarchies between death and rebirth one must be able to behold, to confront these beings consciously. Pictorially speaking, one can wander in darkness, without light (spiritual light, of course) through this realm, through the experiences one should have in the presence of the beings of the higher hierarchies.

The journey can also be accomplished in such a way that, according to the necessities of our karma, the gifts are illumined so that we receive them in the right manner. The light that illumines so that we do not tread in darkness through the realm of the higher hierarchies can never be kindled once we have crossed the gate of death, unless we bring it with us by virtue of the feelings and thoughts towards the higher worlds that we have developed on earth. We ourselves have to prepare it in this life before our physical death. The light is prepared by the thoughts and feelings that we direct, even if only tentatively, towards the supersensible worlds. This light can shine forth only from ourselves—the light that enables us to pass the beings of the higher hierarchies so that they can rightly hand their gifts to us, so that we do not fail to grasp what we should receive.

So we see that the saying that we can wait and need not concern ourselves with the supersensible world until after death is totally untrue. It is absolutely incorrect for the way in which the hierarchies approach us. Whether we encounter them so that we can receive the forces that we need for a next life depends on our being able to illumine a particular area along the journey between death and a new birth. We remain in darkness if we have denied or turned completely away from the idea of the spiritual world until the moment of physical death.

The accepted view may appear plausible, but in the light of higher worlds it is no longer valid. Supersensible perception often reveals that a person who has failed to occupy himself with higher worlds, who has turned away from them and lived exclusively with his thoughts and feelings directed towards the physical world, goes through darkness and misses the gifts that he should have received from the higher hierarchies. When such a soul enters a new earthly existence through birth he lacks certain forces that would have enabled him to fashion his bodily constitution, to form it plastically from within so that he be adequately equipped according to his karma. If a person has dulled himself to the supersensible world in a previous incarnation in the manner indicated, then in a new life he will be ill-equipped and weak. He will have failed to fashion forces in his physical constitution that he should have had at his disposal during his next earthly life; certain inner formations will be lacking. He will be in a certain sense retarded in relation to what he might have been—indeed, to what he should have been. He was dull in a previous life and he will become of necessity duller in the next than he need or should have been. He will not be able to understand as much as he might otherwise have grasped. He will not be able to participate in the life of the world as he otherwise could have done and he will remain disinterested in what otherwise should have interested him.

This may be the result of an obdurate dullness in a previous earth existence. Thus an individual may cross the gate of death again with a soul content that is far below the level of what he could have attained. One might well imagine that when such a person again enters the spiritual world and again journeys between death and rebirth, his forces are even more dimmed, he becomes still more incapable and he wanders in even greater darkness. One might well despair and think that such a person will never find an upward path again but that is not so. Something else intervenes between death and rebirth, a second aspect that we should consider.

In the existence following the life when the individual was of necessity dull, Lucifer and his powers have particularly strong influence, and it is Lucifer who now illumines an area between death and rebirth. He must now receive the gifts of the higher beings illumined by the luciferic powers. As a result, these gifts are endowed with a special coloring. The person who has not gone through darkness, yet is unable to illumine the particular area independently out of his own forces, is capable in the next life of forming plastically what he receives through heredity. Everything that he thus fashions is luciferically colored. When we then observe such a person during his next life we find that he bears the characteristics of many people we meet, especially in our time. These individuals possess a prosaic, dry and egoistic capacity for judgment, and are endowed with a selfish intellect that seeks only its own advantage. These soul characteristics are the result of what has been described previously. Clever egoists who are inclined only to place their cleverness at the service of their own selfish motives are mostly souls who have traveled the path that has been outlined above. Because such souls are no longer dull but are endowed with a variety of forces from earlier incarnations, a further opportunity is given them to bring a ray from the supersensible world into their new earth existence.

In such a way the possibility arises for such souls to be fired with a knowledge of higher worlds. They need not be debarred from further entry into the spiritual world, but have the possibility of climbing upwards again. Here we have a remarkable and important connection between three earthly lives and the two intervening periods between death and rebirth.

Supersensible perception discovers—particularly when it directs its gaze towards contemporaries who are said to be clever, but who act exclusively to their own advantage —that such souls follow a particular pattern. First, an existence during which the soul turns away from all interest in the supersensible world. Second, a life of limited ability because the soul lacks the necessary inner physical organs to take an interest even in its immediate physical surroundings (unless it was in some way predisposed this way).

Third, this is followed by a life that serves only a selfish intellect, an egoistic intelligence. We are able to trace the path of such individuals precisely because selfish intelligence is so widespread in our time. It leads us back to a period in which we find a multitude of people who in a previous incarnation, because of insufficient development, manifested a dull interest in their surroundings. Then we find a third incarnation that for many souls took place during the fourth post-Atlantean period when more atheism and lack of interest for the spiritual world prevailed in many parts of the world than is currently believed today. Because of the particular circumstances of our time it is possible to study the path of development of the soul as characterized above, but this study also plainly reveals the lot of the soul who in our time willfully shuts himself off from supersensible worlds.

A sequence of three earthly lives may take its course in yet another way. The following may occur. We observe a soul who, gripped by a certain fanaticism, satisfies its own strivings, a soul who reveals a religious, egoistic element. We find such souls today. There have always been such souls in the course of the evolution of humanity on the earth, souls who are instinctively endowed with a certain faith because of an inner egoism that awaits a kind of retribution or compensation for earthly life in the world beyond. Such an expectation may be thoroughly egoistic and connected with a fanatic narrow-mindedness in relation to what is imparted to humanity by spiritual science or the Mysteries. There are many people today who hold fast to the possibility of insight into the spiritual world, but who reject fanatically, in a narrow-minded way, anything that is contrary to the confession in which they were born and brought up. Such souls are usually too easy-going to learn to know anything about the spiritual world and although they believe in a beyond, they harbor a profound egoism.

A configuration of this nature indicates again that the soul cannot find the correct path between death and rebirth. The gifts of the beings of the higher hierarchies cannot be received rightly. They work in such a way that, although he can fashion his bodily constitution and partly participate in the formation of his karma, nothing fits properly. He becomes, for example, a hypochondriac, a hypersensitive person who is destined by his mere physical organization to be so affected by his surroundings that he goes through life with a morose, dissatisfied, discontented disposition. Life impinges upon him and he feels continually wounded. The reason a person is a hypochondriac, a pathologically melancholy individual, may be found in what has been described. It is prepared and predestined through the physical organization. When such a soul again goes through the portal of death, supersensible investigation reveals that he falls strongly under the influence of the Ahrimanic forces. These forces now color what a man gathers between death and rebirth and in the next incarnation without his intervention he is so predisposed in his thoughts and feelings as to be narrow-minded. He is incapable of looking at the world in an open, unbiased way. Souls in our environment who display a narrow-mindedness, who are incapable in their thinking of going beyond certain limits, who are as if equipped with blinders, who in spite of genuine efforts are limited, owe their karma to the conditions described above.

In order to clarify still further what is meant, let us consider the following instance. In the spring, the first issue of the *Liberal Thinking Calendar of the Free-Thinkers* (Freidenkerkalender) appeared, devoted to the religious education of children. The man responsible for it appears well-meaning and no doubt thoroughly convinced of the truth of what he writes. He develops the following theory. One should give no religious education to children because it is unnatural. For if one allows children to grow up without injecting religious concepts and feelings into them, one notices that they do not come to them of their own accord. This is supposed to demonstrate that it is unnatural to instill such ideas into children because they merely come from outside.

There can be no doubt that adherents of the free-thinker movement receive such ideas with enthusiasm and even consider them to be profound. Yet one need but reflect on the following. It is common knowledge that if a young child were removed to a desert island before he learned to speak, and there grew up without ever hearing the human voice, he would never learn to speak! This shows clearly that children do not learn to speak unless speech comes to them from outside. The good free-thinking preacher would also have to forbid his followers from teaching children how to talk, for speech also is not developed of its own accord. Thus something that appears eminently logical, and that is regarded as profound by a considerable group of people, is nothing but logical nonsense. As soon as one thinks it through it simply does not hold. This is a typical example of a person wearing blinders.

There are many people like that today. Indeed they appear to have a highly developed soul activity but as soon as they have to go beyond a certain field that they have worked out for themselves, everything collapses. They are utterly incapable of going beyond their rigid boundaries. If we look back into previous embodiments of such people, we find two incarnations as described earlier. This can also shed light on the future of the many souls who, because of love of ease and egoism, lock themselves up in a faith the foundations of which they never inquire about. Is it not so that many people today adhere to a faith because they were born into it and are too easy-going to question it? They are—it is perhaps an impossible thought—equally as good Protestants or Catholics as they would have been Moslems had their karma arranged for them to be born in Islam! We have reached the point in the evolution of humanity when souls will lag behind, in a sense, and will be handicapped in a future incarnation unless they are prepared to open their eyes to what can stream from the spiritual worlds today in a variety of ways.

Karmic connections are indeed complex but light is thrown on them by considering some such examples as have here been discussed. In many other ways does the life between death and rebirth, and therefore also the next incarnation, depend on what has happened previously. By means of supersensible cognition, for example, we can follow souls in the spiritual world who have special tasks between death and rebirth. We do not see in all events on the physical plane how supersensible forces continually play in. Materialism is in this respect the most short-sighted of all ideologies. Thus, all therapeutic forces in the air, or healing forces in the water, or other therapeutic influences in our surroundings are only partly explained by means of the current materialistic therapeutic theories. The way in which healing influences such as growth and blossoming forces bring healthy influences to man's physical being depends on whether the higher hierarchies send their powers of well-being from the supersensible into the sense-perceptible world. All growth and blossoming manifestations, every breath of healthy air—this can be perceived by supersensible perception—is brought about by means of supersensible forces directed by beings of higher hierarchies. The seer can perceive how during a particular phase of life between death and rebirth the human soul becomes the servant of these beings of the higher hierarchies whose task it is to send healthful forces, powers of growth and healing, from the supersensible into the physical world. We can perceive many souls dedicated for a time to the service of such activity between death and rebirth. Souls who are called upon to serve the beings of the higher hierarchies in this way experience a profound blessedness as a result.

Whether a human soul is called upon to become the servant of the good powers as described above depends on whether the soul concerned has accomplished certain specific deeds during his physical incarnation. There are people who inwardly growl at every action they have to perform and are weighed down by the yoke of duty. They may be conscientious, yet everything they do lacks real devotion, enthusiasm and love for the task at hand. Others, on the contrary, bring warmth and enthusiasm to their deeds and are permeated by the feeling that what they do serves a social purpose which profits mankind at large.

Another aspect should be considered in this connection that is of particular importance, especially in our day and age. As compared with ancient times conditions have changed radically. Activities that do not inspire enthusiasm are on the increase. This is a necessary trend in the progressive development of humanity. Indeed, a person should not be deterred from fulfilling his duty, even against his will, if his karma has placed him in a certain situation. Yet every person, if he really has the will, or at least when he is given the opportunity to act, can do something in the course of his life with real devotion providing his karma does not entirely preclude it. Those who have an insight into such matters should realize that they bear a special responsibility in the difficult social conditions of our time. They should do everything in their power to devote themselves to a social activity that can in some way alleviate the burdens borne by those whose lives do not inspire enthusiasm. Souls who are dulled by the prevalent social darkness should be given the opportunity, even if only for a brief span, to accomplish something with enthusiasm, be it only in the sphere of thinking. This is reason enough to be ever more pleased at the expansion of our anthroposophical movement, that it takes root in the social sphere and goes out as a call to the man in the street who might otherwise pursue his life totally unaware that he can in fact think and feel in such a way that he can accomplish something with enthusiasm. It is our task to fire people's enthusiasm.

Our work will become ever more effective in this sphere as time goes on. The connection between earthly existence and life between death and rebirth throws a special light on this thought. Everything we are able to accomplish on earth with devotion, with love for the task at hand so that we are completely involved in what we do and realize that what we do is worthy of man, contributes to making us after death servants of the spiritual beings of the higher hierarchies who send healing, constructive forces from the spiritual into the physical world. This shows the importance of enthusiasm in man's deeds here in the physical world. If enthusiasm were to fade away in the physical world, if love were to die, mankind in the future would enter a physical existence with less healthful and constructive forces from supersensible realms than at present. Because of what is often an unconscious fear, people who turn away from a spiritual conception of the world today prefer to ignore connections between the physical and supersensible worlds. Yet connections between a moral and physical world-order do exist.

The opposite situation should also be considered. We find souls who for a certain period between death and rebirth have to become the servants of spiritual beings who, on the contrary, foster disease and bring misfortune from the supersensible into the physical world. It is a shattering experience to behold souls between death and rebirth who are forced to become the servants of evil spirits of disease and premature death, evil spirits of a gruesome human destiny conditioned by karma by means of external events. That we suffer such a fate depends on our karma. That the external circumstances, however, are so arranged in the sense-perceptible world that we suffer such a fate—this comes about by means of forces directed from the supersensible world. Diseases and epidemics that sweep the world are meant here because in respect to their external occurrence they are directed by supersensible powers, and so are premature deaths.

We have often spoken of death in old age that has to occur with the same necessity as that the leaves of a plant must wither when the seed has been formed for the next plant. Such a death comes about after a ripe life, but death

233

can also strike a man in his early years. When death strikes a man in the bloom of life the conditions are brought about by certain beings of the higher hierarchies who, to begin with, serve a retrogressive element. They send forces into the world that bring about premature deaths, disease and karmic misfortune. It is indeed, as has already been mentioned, a shattering sight to behold souls after death who for a certain period serve beings who bring about illness and death and an evil karma in human existence. Yet, although such a contemplation causes sombre, painful feelings in us, we sense nevertheless a compensation when we trace back the lives of such souls and find the causes for their condition in an earlier physical existence. We do in fact discover that souls who in a previous earth life were lacking in conscience and did not strictly adhere to the truth become the servants of disease and premature deaths. That is one form of compensation, but a rather sombre one.

There are yet other forms that demonstrate that the dark, sombre, compensatory measures that are woven into the web of human existence have their justification in the overall wisdom of the world. Even if an oppressive feeling takes hold of us as a result of certain phenomena, we can nevertheless sense a definite relief when we consider its counterpart in the overall structure of existence. For instance, when a person dies prematurely as a result of an accident or because of illness, we find that such souls are still endowed after death with forces that otherwise would have sustained their earthly sheaths. They carry these forces upward into a higher spiritual realm after death. Such souls encounter the supersensible worlds differently from others who have lived out their earthly existence.

It is important to observe such souls after death and to

follow their further existence. They carry into the higher worlds forces that normally would have served a physical earthly existence. What happens to these forces?

These forces are used to a most beautiful end in the supersensible world. The beings of the higher hierarchies who guide and ordain the progressive course of evolution are endowed with certain forces that make this course possible. This is not due to an imperfection in the universe but it depends on certain other perfect factors, for all forces, even those of the higher hierarchies are to some extent limited, are not infinite. We discover that there are already souls today who, when they enter the spiritual world after death, are so constituted that the spirits of the higher hierarchies who foster progressive evolution cannot do anything with them. I have often emphasized that there are souls today who are in no way inclined to develop an understanding of the supersensible worlds in accordance with our day and age, who are thoroughly materialistic and who have completely cut themselves off from the spiritual world. It is precisely such souls who after death make it difficult for the beings of the spiritual hierarchies to do anything with them. These spiritual beings of the higher hierarchies possess forces destined for the progressive course of evolution. Souls who have closed themselves completely against this progressive course are also too heavy, so heavy in fact that the beings of the higher hierarchies cannot overcome the weight. We need not despair today in respect to such souls. The real danger point will occur in the sixth post-Atlantean epoch, and ultimately they will be totally cast off from progressive evolution during the Venus period. If, however, nothing else were to intervene, such souls would have to be cast off earlier from progressive evolution because they would be totally useless to the beings of the higher hierarchies.

It is in fact so that obstacles arise against the challenge of progressive evolution that sounds forth to mankind. A considerable number of human beings in our time are as yet unable to find a deep feeling relationship to the Christ impulse even though the earth has reached a stage of development when the human soul needs the Christ impulse if it is to go through life between death and rebirth in the right way. Souls who go through the gate of death without some connection with the Christ impulse are in danger because the leaders of progress, the beings of the higher hierarchies, are unable to bring their forces to bear on souls who have torn themselves out of the stream of evolution and who, as a result of their strange existence, destine themselves to ruin. The beings of the higher hierarchies are only able to make something of this situation by virtue of the fact that the forces of souls who have died prematurely flow toward the higher hierarchies. Thereby forces that have not been made use of, forces that could still have been used on earth but no longer serve the need of physical existence because the body has been cast off prematurely, flow upwards to the spiritual world.

Consider how many souls have entered the spiritual worlds as a result of catastrophes such as the sinking of the *Titanic* or the earthquake of Messina, consider the considerable numbers of souls who in recent times have died in all parts of the world before their lives had run their courses under normal circumstances. Then reflect on the many forces that could have been used for earthly existence that as a result flowed upwards into higher worlds! These forces increase the powers of the higher hierarchies, which otherwise would not be sufficient to lead souls who exclude themselves from the progressive course of evolution back into the progressive stream.

We must, of course, live out our karma. Attention must be drawn to this fact in discussing such a matter. It would be a most sinful deed against the wisdom-filled guidance of the universe if a man were to decide to do something himself in order to become a servant of human progress by virtue of unused forces so as to help souls who are in danger of being cast off. A man should not undertake anything in this direction. If, however, his karma fulfills itself so that he dies prematurely, he thereby becomes a servant of the beings of the higher hierarchies in the noblest, most blessed manner. These unused forces can then be employed to save souls who would otherwise have been lost. That is the beautiful goal of souls who die in the flower of their existence. In spite of the sorrow that fills us when we experience the premature death of someone, such thoughts can bring comfort. At moments such as these we can acquire a wider survey of the wisdom-filled guidance of the universe.

Indeed, how amazing is the cycle of events when we behold it spiritually. On the one hand we have souls who through their lack of conscience prepare themselves to send illnesses, premature deaths and accidents into our world. On the other hand, are those souls who fall ill, are stricken by premature death and are involved in accidents. This offers the opportunity for the karma of a lack of conscience to be lived out. Such observations weigh heavily on one's soul and are among the most gruesome that can be made by the seer when he penetrates into the deeper connections of existence.

One often imagines insight into the spiritual world as a

blessed condition. This is true for certain realms but when one penetrates into the mysteries of still higher realms much of what one beholds there fills one with a feeling of horror. The seer is moved most deeply and a considerable call is thereby made on his own forces when karmic connections of human beings reveal themselves to his supersensible gaze—providing, of course, such investigaions are made thoroughly and conscientiously without any form of idle speculation.

But then again we recognize, even when the most gruesome and horrible matters are involved, how wisdom-filled the overall guidance is!

We behold the fate of souls lacking in conscience and how this leads to conditions of illness and premature deaths brought about from the spiritual into the physical world. On the other hand, we behold those who suffer, who are involved in premature death and who thereby increase forces that are destined for healing, for the saving of mankind, forces that otherwise would not be available.

This indeed is a wonderful, redeeming aspect. On the one hand, the possibility to err must be present, to approach because of human error the dangerous condition of being cast out from the stream of evolution. If that were not possible, man could not accomplish his mission on earth. On the other hand, the other possibility of which we have spoken today also exists and it is also part of the earth evolution that certain people die in the flower of youth. Supersensible vision sees that the beings of the higher hierarchies rely on such souls to send forces for the healing and redemption of humanity that otherwise would not be available.

We can feel reconciled to such facts when we consider

238

that a wisdom-filled cosmic guidance needs certain gruesome situations in order to accomplish deeds inspired by a
still loftier wisdom. It is utterly nonsensical to ask whether
the spiritual powers might not have created a pleasant existence for all men and all beings in the universe without
such detours. One who has such a wish might be compared
to one who considers the work of the gods quite imperfect
because they have ordained that a circle cannot be a square.
One might not at once realize that both statements have
the same inherent value, and yet it is so. Just as there can
be no light without darkness, so there also cannot be a
mighty, light-filled impulse that streams upward from unused forces on earth into the spiritual worlds unless the
karma of certain souls lacking in conscience were to take
its course.

Such considerations make it clear that when we are
tempted to discover imperfections in the universe or in
man's surroundings, we should permeate ourselves with
the feeling that finding fault is based on a lack of insight
that does not enable us to survey the total web of connections. Whenever we are tempted to criticize the imperfections of existence, we make a step forward if we consider
this attitude due to a shortcoming in ourselves. Even if
one experiences sorrow it is best never to resort in one's
suffering to criticize the wise guidance of the universe, but
rather to say to oneself that where a lack of wisdom appears
in the universe it is due to maya. Maya, the great illusion
that spreads a veil because we are not able to penetrate to
the full reality of things.

Thus much light can be shed on physical earth existence
when we turn our gaze to the area that man traverses between death and rebirth. Physical existence is not only

penetrated by supersensible influences, the deeds that man accomplishes between death and rebirth also stream downwards to the earth. Much of what occurs on earth, much of what meets a person, is brought about in a variety of ways by forces that human souls develop between death and rebirth. The activity of souls who go through the gate of death with unused forces, about which we have heard, is among the noblest that can be accomplished.

XIII

LIFE BETWEEN DEATH AND REBIRTH

Man's Journey through the Cosmic Spheres after Death

Munich, March 12, 1913

D URING my last visit here I spoke about man's life between death and rebirth and how that life is connected with the great realm of the cosmos. I wanted to show how the path traversed by the human being between death and a new birth actually leads through the cosmic spheres. Let us now briefly recapitulate what was said then.

The first period after a man's death is filled with experiences connected in some way with his recent life on earth. He is emerging from, growing away from, his last earthly life, and during the first period after death the emotions, passions and feelings that affected his astral body all continue to exist. Because during physical incarnation man is conscious of these feelings only when he is actually within his physical body, it is natural that his experiences of all these forces in the astral body is essentially different when he is passing through the region of existence between death and a new birth. In normal cases, although there are many exceptions, a sense of deprivation is present during the first period after death. This is due to the fact that man must live through the experiences in his astral body without having a physical body at his disposal. He still longs for his physical body, and in normal cases this longing holds him back in the sphere of the earth for a longer or shorter period. Life in kamaloca takes its course in the sphere between the earth and the orbit of the moon, but experiences in kamaloca that are of essential significance take place in a realm nearer the earth than, let us say, the orbit of the moon.

Souls who have unfolded only few feelings and sentiments transcending the affairs of earthly life remain bound to the earth sphere by their own cravings for a considerable time. Even outwardly it is easy to understand that a man who for a whole lifetime has cultivated only such feelings as can be satisfied by means of bodily organs and earthly conditions can but remain bound to the earth sphere for a certain time. Impulses and desires quite different from those ordinarily imagined can also cause a soul to remain bound to the earth sphere. Ambitious people, for instance, who cultivate an inordinate longing for certain things within earthly conditions and who depend on the appreciation of their fellow men, thereby develop an emotional disturbance in their astral body that will result in their being bound to the earth sphere for a longer time after death. There are many reasons for which human souls are held back in the earth sphere. By far the greater majority of communications from the spirit world made by mediums stem from such souls and consist essentially of what they are striving to cast off.

Although the motives binding these souls to the earth are mostly ignoble, it need not invariably be so. It may also be due to anxiety for those who have been left behind on earth. Concern for friends, relatives and children may also act as a kind of gravity that holds souls back in the earth sphere. It is important to pay attention to this because by taking it into account we can also help the dead. If, for instance, we realize that the departed soul feels anxiety for a living person—and much can come to our knowledge in this respect—it will help the dead person in his further development to relieve him of this anxiety. We ease the life of someone who has died by relieving him, for example, of anxiety about a child whom he has left behind unprovided for. By doing something for the child, we relieve the dead person of anxiety, and this is a true service of love. Let us picture such a situation. The dead person has not available the means to rid himself of anxiety. From his realm he may be unable to do anything that would ease the circumstances of a child, a relative or a friend. He is often condemned— and in many cases this weighs heavily upon the seer—to bear the anxiety until the situation of the one left behind improves of itself or by circumstances. Therefore, if we do something to better the situation we will have performed a real deed of love for the dead one.

It has frequently been observed that a person who had planned to do something definite in life died and then continued to cling to the plan after his death. We help him if we ourselves attempt to do what he would have liked to do. These situations are not difficult to grasp. We should take account of them because they tally with clairvoyant observation.

There are many other facts that may keep a soul in the etheric sphere of the earth. Eventually he grows beyond this sphere. This process has already partly been described. Our concepts must be recast if we wish to gain an understanding of the life between death and rebirth. It is not really incongruous to speak about the dead in words taken from the conditions of earthly existence because our language is adapted to these conditions. Although what can be expressed in words about life after death tallies only in a pictorial sense, it need not necessarily be incorrect.

Descriptions are never quite accurate that convey the idea that the dead are confined to a definite place like a being who is living in a physical body. What is experienced both after death and in initiation is that one is emerging from the body and one's whole soul-being is expanding. When we follow a soul who has reached the Moon sphere as we call it, the "body" denotes the expansion of the range of experience. In actual fact the human being grows, in a spiritual sense, to gigantic dimensions. He grows out into the spheres, but the spheres of the dead are not separate from each other as in the case of men on earth. They are spatially intermingled. A sense of separateness arises because consciousness is separate. Beings may be completely intermingled without knowing anything of one another.

The feeling of either isolation or community after death of which I spoke during my last visit is connected with the interrelationships of consciousness. It is not as if a dead person were on some isolated island in a spatial sense. He pervades the other being of whose existence he is totally unaware although they occupy the same space.

Let us now consider what comes about mainly when the period of kamaloca is over. When an individual enters upon his devachanic existence after passing through the Moon sphere, kamaloca is not yet entirely at an end. This does not preclude the fact that it is within the Moon sphere that adjustments take place that are of significance not only as kamaloca experiences, but also for the later life of the individual when he again enters existence through birth. We can characterize in the following way what is added to the kamaloca experiences. A man may be so active in life that he brings all his talents to expression. But there are many men of whom we have to say, when we observe them with the eyes of the soul, that according to their faculties and talents they could have achieved in life something quite different from what they have in fact achieved. Such people have lagged behind their talents.

Something else comes into consideration. There are people who nurture a great number of intentions in the course of their life. It need not be a question of talent, but of intentions connected either with trivial or important aims. How much in life merely remains at the stage of intention without being fulfilled!

There are things in this category that need not be considered blameworthy. In order to show how significant such things may be I will mention an instance already known to some friends. Goethe embarked in his *Pandora* upon a poetical work and at a certain point he came to a standstill. I once explained what happened to Goethe when writing *Pandora* in the following way. The very greatness that had conceived the plan of the poem prevented him from completing the work. He was incapable of unfolding the power whereby the plan could have turned into reality. It was not because of shortcomings but in a sense because of his greatness that Goethe was prevented from completing *Pandora*. This is the case with some of his other works, too. He left them unfinished. The fragment of *Pandora* shows that Goethe made such considerable artistic demands upon himself that his powers, even in respect of the outer form of the poem, were simply not able to carry out the entire mighty plan with the same ease as in the fragment with which he was successful. This is obviously an example of an unfulfilled intention.

Therefore, on the one hand, a man may lag behind his talents owing to laziness or to defects in character or intellect, but the other possibility is that he may not be able to carry out his intentions in small or important matters. Now there is something great in a poet who does not complete a work such as *Pandora,* but every imperfection in man is inscribed by him into the Akasha Chronicle in the Moon sphere, and thus an abundance of shortcomings and imperfections come before the eye of the seer in the realm between Earth and Moon. Human imperfections, be they noble or no, are faithfully recorded there. Instances can be found in which, through physical health, through a bodily constitution providing a good foundation for intellectual gifts, a man would have been capable of achieving certain things, but failed to do so. What he could have become but had not become when he passed through the gate of death—this is inscribed in the Akasha Chronicle.

Do not imagine that the end of *Pandora* is in some way inscribed in the Moon sphere. What is inscribed has to do with Goethe's astral body, namely, that he had conceived a great, far-reaching plan and only fulfilled a part of it. All such things, including trivial matters, are inscribed between the spheres of Earth and Moon. A person who forms a resolution but has not carried it out before his death, inscribes the fact of non-fulfillment in this sphere. A fairly accurate characterization can be given of what is disclosed to the eye of seership in this realm. A promise that has not been kept, for example, is not inscribed until later, actually not until the Mercury sphere is reached. An unfulfilled resolution, however, is inscribed in the Moon sphere. Anything that affects not only ourselves but also others is not immediately inscribed in the Moon sphere, but only later. Anything that affects us as individuals, that keeps us behind our proper stage of evolution and thus denotes imperfection in our personal development, is inscribed in the Moon sphere.

It is important to realize that our imperfections, especially those that need not have been inevitable, are inscribed in the Moon sphere.

It should not be thought that in all circumstances such an inscription is a dreadful thing. In a certain sense it can be of the greatest value and significance. We will speak in a moment of the meaning and purpose of these inscriptions in the Akasha Chronicle. First it must be emphasized that as the person expands into other spheres, all his imperfections are there inscribed. He expands from the Moon sphere into the Mercury sphere; I am speaking entirely from the aspect of occultism, not from that of ordinary astronomy. Something is inscribed by him in all the spheres, in the Mercury sphere, the Venus sphere, the Sun sphere, the Mars sphere, the Jupiter sphere, the Saturn sphere and even beyond.

Most inscriptions, however, are made within the Sun sphere, for as we heard in the last lecture, outside the Sun sphere a man mainly has to adjust matters that are not just left to his own individual discretion.

Thus after having cast away more or less completely what still draws him to the earth, man journeys through the planetary spheres and even beyond them. The contact thus established with the corresponding forces provides what he needs in his evolution between death and a new birth. When I spoke in the last lecture of man coming into contact with the higher hierarchies and receiving the gifts they bestow, that was the same as saying that his being expands into the cosmos. When the expansion has been completed he contracts again until he has become minute enough to unite as a spirit-seed with what comes from the parents. This is indeed a wonderful mystery. When the human being passes through the gate of death he himself becomes an ever-expanding sphere. His potentialities of soul and spirit expand. He becomes a gigantic being and then again contracts. What we have within us has in fact contracted from the planetary universe. Quite literally we bear within us what we have lived through in a planetary world.

When I was here last I said certain things about the passage through the Mercury sphere, the Venus sphere and the Sun sphere. Today I wish to speak about certain aspects of the passage through the Mars sphere. When a man passes from the Sun sphere into the Mars sphere, the conditions of existence into which he enters are quite different in our present age from what they were a comparatively short time ago. To the eyes of the seer it is quite evident that there was good reason for the statements, originating from the clairvoyance once possessed by humanity, about the several bodies composing the planetary system. It was entirely in keeping with the facts that Mars was considered to be the member of our planetary system connected with all warlike, aggressive elements in the evolution of humanity. The fantastic theories advanced by physical astronomy today about a possible form of life on Mars are without foundation. The nature of the beings who may be called "Mars men," if we wish to use such an expression, is altogether different from that of the men on earth, and no comparison is possible. Until the seventeenth century the character of the Mars beings had invariably been one of warlike aggressiveness.

Belligerency, if one may use this word, was an inherent quality of the Mars "culture." The basis of it was formed by the rivalries and clashes between souls perpetually battling with each other. As an individual was passing through the Mars sphere between death and rebirth, he came into contact with these forces of aggression and they made their way into his soul. If when he was born again his innate tendencies made him specially able to develop and give expression to these forces, it was to be attributed to his passage through the Mars sphere.

This subject is full of complications. On the earth we live among the beings of the three kingdoms of nature, and among men. By various means we come into contact with the souls who in their life after death still retain some connection with the earth but we also encounter beings who are utterly foreign to the earth. The more an initiate is able to widen his vision, the more souls are found who are strangers on the earth, and the more it is realized that wanderers are passing through the earth sphere. They are beings who are not connected with earthly life in the normal way. This is no different for us as men of earth than it is for the moon dwellers through whose sphere of life we also pass between death and a new birth. When we are passing through the Mars sphere, for example, we are ghosts, spectres, for the Mars dwellers. We pass through their sphere as strangers, as alien beings. But the Mars beings, too, at a certain stage of their existence, are condemned to pass through our earth sphere and one who possesses certain initiate faculties encounters them when conditions are favorable.

Beings of our planetary system are continually streaming past each other. While we are living on earth, often imagining that we are surrounded only by the beings of the different kingdoms of nature, there are itinerants from all the other planets in our environment. During a certain period between death and a new birth we, too, are itinerants among the other planetary "men," if one might speak in this way. We have to develop in our lives on earth the essentials of our particular mission in the present epoch of cosmic existence. Other beings are alloted to the other planetary worlds, and between death and rebirth we must contact these worlds, too. Therefore, when reference is made to one region or another of life in Devachan, it is actually the case, although it is not expressly stated, that the happenings are taking place in some sphere of our planetary system. This should be borne in mind. Thus at a certain time in life between death and a new birth we pass through the Mars sphére.

Just as the process of the earth evolution is a process of descent until the time of the Mystery of Golgotha, and of ascent from then onwards, so also do the other planets undergo an evolution in their own way. From the year 33 A.D., the date is approximately correct, the earth entered upon an ascending process of evolution. That year was the pivotal point in the earth's evolution. On Mars the pivotal point was at the beginning of the seventeenth century. Until then, the evolution of conditions on Mars had been a process of descent and from that time onwards a process of ascent has occurred because an event of the greatest significance for that planet then took place.

In connection with earth evolution we know of the remarkable personage, Gautama Buddha. He was a Bodhisattva until in the twenty-ninth year of his life he rose to the rank of Buddhahood and was then destined never to be incarnated again in a physical body on earth. From other lectures you will have heard, however, that later on the Buddha still worked into the earth sphere from the spiritual world. He sent his forces into the astral body of the Jesus child of the Gospel of St. Luke. But in another way, too, he influenced earthly life without incarnating into a physical body. In the seventh and eighth centuries there was a mystery school in the southeast of Europe for those who at that time were endowed with some degree of seership. The teachers in that school were not only individualities in physical incarnation but there were also those who work from spiritual heights only as far as the etheric body. It is possible for more highly developed men to receive instruction from individualities who no longer, or never, descend into a physical body. The Buddha himself was a teacher in the mystery school. Among his pupils at that time was the personality who was born later on in his next incarnation as Francis of Assisi. Many of the qualities so impressively displayed in that later life are to be traced to the fact that Francis of Assisi had been a pupil of the Buddha.

Here we see how the Buddha continued to work from spiritual heights into the earth sphere after the Mystery of Golgotha, and how he was connected with the life of man between birth and death.

Then, in the seventeenth century, the Buddha withdrew from earthly existence and accomplished for Mars a deed that, although not of the magnitude of the Mystery of Golgotha, nevertheless resembled it and corresponded on Mars to the Mystery of Golgotha on earth. At the beginning of the seventeenth century the Buddha became the redeemer, the savior of Mars. He was the individuality whose mission it was to inculcate peace and harmony into the aggressive nature of Mars. Since then the Buddha impulse is to be found on Mars, as the Christ impulse is to be found on the earth since the Mystery of Golgotha.

The destiny of the Buddha on Mars was not death as in the Mystery of Golgotha. Yet in a certain respect it, too, was a kind of crucifixion inasmuch as this wonderful individuality, who in keeping with his life on earth radiated universal peace and love, was transferred into the midst of what was completely alien to him, into the aggressive, warlike element on Mars. It was Buddha's mission to exercise a pacifying influence on Mars. For the gaze of seership there is something tremendously impressive in the picture of two collateral events. The Buddha had risen to the highest point attainable in his earthly existence, to the rank of Buddhahood, and had lived on earth as the Buddha for fifty years. Then in his eightieth year, on October 13, 483 B.C., on a glorious moonlit night, he breathed out his being into the silvery radiance glimmering over the earth. This event, which even outwardly seems to be a manifestation of the breath of peace emanating from the Buddha, bears witness to the fact that he had attained the zenith of development within his earthly existence. It is deeply impressive to contemplate this wonderful happening in connection with that moment at the beginning of the seventeenth century when, with all his abounding powers of peace and love, the Buddha went to Mars in order that those powers might stream from him into the aggressiveness prevailing there to gradually inaugurate the process of Mars' ascending evolution.

When a soul passed through the Mars sphere in times before the Buddha Mystery, it was endowed primarily with forces of aggressiveness. Since the Buddha Mystery a soul undergoes essentially different experiences if it is fitted by nature to gain something from the Mars forces. To avoid any misunderstanding it must be emphasized that as little as the whole earth today is already Christianized, as little has Mars become entirely a planet of peace. That process will still take a long time so that if a soul has any aptitude for receiving elements of aggressiveness there is still ample opportunity for it. Nevertheless, we must not lose sight, spiritually, of the event of which we have spoken. The more deeply the earth enters into a phase of materialism, the less will anyone who really understands the evolutionary process admit that it would be natural for a man in his life between birth and death to follow Buddha in the way that men followed him in pre-Christian times. The development of natures such as that of Francis of Assisi will gradually become less and less possible on earth, less and less suitable for external civilization. Nevertheless, between death and rebirth the soul is able to pass through this experience. Grotesque as it may seem, yet it corresponds to the facts, for a certain period between death and a new birth, during the passage through the Mars sphere, every human soul has the opportunity of being a Franciscan or a Buddhist and of receiving all the forces that can flow from feeling and experience of this kind. The passage through the Mars sphere can therefore be of great importance for the human soul. Man, however, inscribes his perfections and imperfections into whatever sphere he enters according to their affiniy with the characteristic qualities of that sphere.

Between death and rebirth our perfections and imperfections are faithfully recorded in the Akasha Chronicle. Certain attributes are inscribed in the Moon sphere, others in the Venus sphere, others in the Mars sphere, others in the Mercury sphere, others in the Jupiter sphere, and so on. When we are returning to an incarnation in a physical body and our being is slowly contracting, we encounter everything that was inscribed on the outward journey. In this way our karma is prepared. On the path of return we can inscribe into our own being the record of an imperfection we ourselves first inscribed into the Akasha Chronicle. Then we arrive on the earth. Because there is within us everything we inscribed into our being on the return journey, and we are obliged to inscribe a great deal even if not everything, because of this our karma unfolds. Up above, however, everything still remains inscribed.

Now these inscriptions work together in a remarkable way. They are engraved into the spheres, into the Moon sphere, Venus sphere, and so on. These spheres are involved in certain movements so that the following may happen. Let us say that a man has inscribed one of his imperfections into the Moon sphere. While passing through the Mars sphere he has inscribed there a quality of his character through the fact that he acquired in that sphere a certain element of aggressiveness that was not previously in him. Now on the return journey he passes through the Mars sphere again and comes back to the earth. He lives on the earth and has received into his karma what he has inscribed in the Mars sphere but at the same time it stands recorded above him. Up there is Mars, in a certain relationship to the Moon. (The outer planets indicate the relative positions of the spheres.) Because Mars stands in a certain relationship to the Moon, the inscription of the aggressive element and the man's imperfections are, as it were, in the same constellation. The consequence is that when the one planet stands behind the other they work in conjunction. This is the time when the individual in question will tackle his imperfection with the aggressive quality acquired from Mars. So the position of the planets really does indicate what the man himself has first inscribed into these spheres.

When in astrology we ascertain the positions of the planets and also their relative positions to those of the fixed stars, this gives some indication of what we ourselves have inscribed. The outer planets are in this case a less important factor. What actually has an effect upon us is what we ourselves have inscribed in the several spheres. Here is the real reason why the planetary constellations have an effect upon man's nature. It is because he actually passes through the several planetary spheres. When the Moon stands in a certain relationship to Mars and to some fixed star, this constellation works as a whole. That is to say, the Mars quality, Moon and fixed star work in conjunction upon the man and bring about what this combined influence is able to achieve.

So it is really the moral inheritance deposited by us between death and rebirth that appears again in a new life as a stellar constellation in our karma. That is the deeper basis of the connection between the stellar constellation and man's karma. Thus if we study the life of a man between death and a new birth we perceive how significantly he is connected with the whole cosmos.

An element of necessity enters into a man's connection with the realms lying beyond the Sun sphere. Let us consider the Saturn sphere in particular. If during his present earth life a man has made efforts to master the concepts of spiritual science, the passage through the Saturn sphere is of special significance for his next life. It is in this sphere that the conditions are created that enable him to transmute the forces acquired through the knowledge of spiritual science or anthroposophy into forces that elaborate his bodily constitution in such a way that in his coming life he has a natural inclination towards the spiritual. A human being may grow up today and be educated as a materialist, Protestant or Catholic. Spiritual science approaches him. He is receptive to it and does not reject it. He inwardly accepts it. He now passes through the gate of death. He enters the Saturn sphere. In passing through it, he absorbs the forces that make him in his next life a spiritual man, who shows even as a child an inclination to the spiritual.

It is the function of every sphere through which we pass between death and rebirth to transform what our souls have assimilated during an incarnation into forces that can then become bodily forces and endow us with certain faculties. Yesterday I could only go as far as is possible in a public lecture when I said that the true Christian impulses were already in Raphael when he was born. This must not be taken to imply that Raphael brought with him some definite Christian concepts or ideas. I have said *impulses*, not *concepts*. What has been taken into the conceptual life in one incarnation is united with the human being in quite a different form. It appears as impulses or forces. The power that enabled Raphael to create those delicate, wonderful figures of Christianity in his paintings came from his earlier incarnations. We are justified in speaking of him as a "born Christian." Most of you know that Raphael had been incarnated previously as John the Baptist, and it was then that the impulses that appeared in the Raphael existence as inborn Christian impulses had penetrated into his soul.

It must always be emphasized that conjectures and comparisons may lead far off the mark when speaking about successive incarnations. To the eyes of seership they present themselves in such a way that in most cases one would not take one life to be the cause of the next. In order that something assimilated in the life of the soul in one incarnation may be able to unfold forces in the next incarnation that work upon the bodily foundation of talents, we must pass through the period from death to rebirth. On earth and with terrestrial forces it is impossible to transform what our souls have experienced in earthly life into forces capable of working upon the bodily constitution itself. Man in his totality is not an earth being, and his physical form would have a grotesque appearance according to modern ideas if only those forces present in the earth sphere could be applied to his bodily development.

When an individual comes into existence through birth he must bear within him the forces of the cosmos, and these forces must continue to work within him if he is to assume human form. Forces that build up and give shape to such forms cannot be found within the earth sphere. This must be borne in mind. Thus in what he is man bears the image of the cosmos in himself, not merely that of the earth. It is a sin against the true nature of man to trace his source and origin to earthly forces, and to study only what can be observed externally in the kingdoms of the earth through natural science. Nor should we ignore the fact that everything a man receives from the earth is dominated by what he brings with him from those super-earthly spheres through which he passes between death and rebirth. Within these several spheres he becomes a servant of one or the other of the higher hierarchies.

What is inscribed in the Akasha Chronicle between the earth and the moon is of special importance because it is there that among other things all imperfections are recorded. It should be realized that the inscribing of these imperfections is governed by the view that every record there is of significance for the individual's own evolution, either furthering or hindering his progress. Because it is there inscribed in the Akasha Chronicle between earth and moon, it also becomes significant for the evolution of the earth as a whole. The imperfections of really great men are also recorded in that sphere. One example of tremendous interest for clairvoyant observation is Leonardo da Vinci. He is a spirit of greatness and universality equalled by few others on earth, but compared with what he intended, his actual achievements in the external world in many respects remained incomplete. As a matter of fact, no man of similar eminence left as much uncompleted as Leonardo da Vinci. The consequence of this was that a colossal amount was inscribed by him in the Moon sphere, so much indeed that one is often bound to exclaim, "How could all that is inscribed there possibly have reached perfection on the earth!"

At this point I want to tell you of something that seemed to me quite significant when I was studying Leonardo da Vinci. I was to give a lecture about him in Berlin and a particular observation made in connection with him seemed to be extremely important. It fills one with sadness today to see on the wall of the Church of Santa Maria della Grazie in Milan the rapidly disappearing colors that now convey no more than a faint shadow of what the picture once was. If we remember that Leonardo took sixteen years to paint this picture, and think of how he painted it, we gain a definite impression. It is known that he would often go away for a long time. Then he would return to the picture, sit in front of it for many hours, make a few strokes with the brush and go off again. It is also known that many times he felt unable to express what he wished in the painting and suffered terrible fits of depression on this account. Now it happened that a new prior was appointed to the monastery at a time when Leonardo had already been working at the picture for many years. This prior was a pedantic and strict disciplinarian with little understanding of art. He asked impatiently why the painter could not finish the picture, reproached him for it and also complained to Duke Ludovico. The Duke repeated the complaint to Leonardo and he answered, "I do not know whether I shall ever be able to complete this picture. I have prototypes in life for all the figures except those of Judas and Christ. For them I have no models, although in the case of Judas if no model turns up I can always take the prior. But for the Christ I have no prototype." That, however, is digressing.

What I want to say is that when one looks today at the figure of Judas in the picture that has almost completely faded, a shadow is to be seen on this figure, a shadow that cannot be explained in any way, either by the instreaming light or by anything else. Occult investigation finds that the painting was never as Leonardo da Vinci really wanted it to be. With the exception of the figures of Judas and the Christ he wanted to portray everything through light and shadow, but Judas was to be portrayed in such a way as to give the impression that darkness dominated the countenance from within. This was not intended to be conveyed by external contrasts of light and shadows. In the figure of Christ the impression was to be that the light on His countenance was shining from within, radiating outwards from within. But at this point disharmony beset Leonardo's inner life, and the effect he desired was never produced.

This affords a clue when one is observing the many remaining inscriptions made by Leonardo in the Moon sphere. It is an example of something that could not be brought to fulfillment in the earth sphere.

When the period following that of Leonardo da Vinci is investigated, it is found that Leonardo continued to work through a number of those who lived after him. Even externally there can be found in Leonardo's writings things that later on were demonstrated by scientists and also by artists. In fact, the whole subsequent period was under his influence. It is then discovered that the inscribed imperfections worked as inspirations into the souls of Leonardo's successors, into the souls of men who lived after him.

The imperfections of an earlier epoch are still more important for the following epoch than its perfections. The perfections are there to be studied, but what has been elaborated to a certain degree of perfection on the earth has, as it were, reached an end, has come to a conclusion in evolution. What has not been perfected is the seed of the following divine evolutionary process. Here we come to a remarkable, magnificent paradox. The greatest blessing for a subsequent period is the fruitful imperfection, the fruitful, justifiable imperfection of an earlier period. What has been perfected in an earlier epoch is there to be enjoyed. Imperfection, however, imperfection originating in great men whose influences have remained for posterity, helps to promote creative activity in the following period. Hence, there is obviously tremendous wisdom in the fact that imperfections remain in the neighborhood of the earth, inscribed in the records of the Akasha Chronicle between earth and moon.

This brings us to the point where we can begin to understand the principle that perfection signifies for the different epochs the end of a stream of evolution, and imperfection, the beginning of an evolutionary stream. For imperfection in this sense men should actually be thankful to the gods.

What is the purpose of studies such as are contained in this lecture? The purpose is to make man's connection with the macrocosm more and more comprehensible, to show how men bear the macrocosm compressed within them and also how they can be related to their spiritual environment. Realization of what these things mean can then be transformed into a feeling that pervades a man in such a way that he combines with this knowledge a concept of his dignity that does not make him arrogant, but fills him with a sense of responsibility, prompts him to believe not that he may squander his powers, but that he must use them.

It must, of course, be emphasized that it would be futile to say, "I had better leave imperfect such faculties as I possess." Nothing whatever could be gained by such an attitude! If a man were deliberately to ignore his imperfections, he would, it is true, inscribe them as described, but they would have no light nor would they be capable of having any effect. Only those imperfections that are inscribed because they were due to necessity and not to result of laziness can work in the way that has been described.

FURTHER FACTS ABOUT LIFE BETWEEN

DEATH AND REBIRTH

Breslau, April 5, 1913

.

XIV

FURTHER FACTS ABOUT LIFE BETWEEN
DEATH AND REBIRTH

Breslau, April 5, 1913

In COMING together in our group meetings we can
speak more precisely about things than is possible in public
lectures and written works. Today I would like to present
supplementary considerations to add to what is to be found
in the books and cycles of lectures.

You can imagine, my dear friends, that life between death
and a new birth is as rich and varied as life here between
birth and death, and that whenever one describes what happens after death one can obviously only deal with certain
aspects. Today I will not touch so much on what is already
known, but draw attention to what can shed further light
upon it.

If one is able to look into the spiritual worlds where man
dwells between death and a new birth, then particularly in
our time the necessity of what is intended with our spiritual
scientific work is confirmed, that is, the need to give something to the hearts and souls of men by way of spiritual
science.

Let us take our starting point from a particular instance.
A man died. He loved his wife deeply and was much attached
to his family. Spiritual observation showed that he suffered

265

deeply from the fact that when he looked down on the earth he was unable to find the souls of his wife and children. Now in the manner by which the seer can enter into communication with a person after death, the man informed the seer that with his thoughts and with all his feelings he was able to relive the time when he was united with his beloved on the earth. But he added, "When I lived on earth my wife was like sunshine to me. Now I must forego this. I am able to direct my thoughts back to what I have experienced but I cannot find my wife."

Why is this? For this is not the case with all who pass through the gate of death. If we were to go back several thousands of years, we would find that the souls of men were able to look down from the spiritual world and participate in the affairs of those who remained behind on the earth. Why was this the case for all souls in ancient times before the Mystery of Golgotha? In ancient times, as you know, men so lived on the earth that they still possessed an original clairvoyance. They not only saw the sense world by means of the eyes. They also gazed into the spiritual origins, into the archetypal beings behind the sense world. The capacity to live with the spiritual world during physical existence brought with it the ability of the soul to perceive what it had left behind on the earth after death. Today souls no longer have the faculty of living directly with the spiritual world because the evolution of humanity has consisted in man's descent into physical existence out of the spiritual world. This has resulted in the faculty of judgment and so forth, but it has robbed man of the faculty to live with the spiritual world.

During a period immediately following the Mystery of

Golgotha when souls were deeply moved by the Christ impulse, at last a part of mankind was able to regain this faculty to some extent. Now, however, we again live in an age when souls who go through the gate of death and have not concerned themselves with the realities of the spirit lose the connection. Mankind needs a spiritual revelation and we can have a justified conviction that it should permeate human souls. Today the old religious confession does not suffice. Souls who seek to gaze down spiritually from the other world to ours need what they can receive by means of a spiritual scientific understanding of the Mystery of Golgotha. It is therefore our endeavor that spirit light may develop in their souls.

The man of whom we have spoken had not concerned himself in any way with thoughts or feelings about the spiritual world. He went through the gate of death but no thoughts of the spiritual world had occupied his mind. He therefore was able to say, "I know by means of my memory that my wife is down there. I know she is there, but I cannot see her, cannot find her."

Under what conditions would he have been able to find her? At the present time only such souls can be perceived in whom spiritual faculties dwell. Such souls can be seen from the other world, souls in whom thoughts live with understanding for the spirit. As the dead one gazes down, a person who has remained behind on the earth only becomes visible for him when spiritual thoughts live within the soul of that person. The dead person sees these thoughts. Otherwise the person remains invisible and the dead one suffers from the anguish of knowing that the person is there but he is unable to find him. As soon as one succeeds in conveying to such a soul thoughts concerning the spiritual world, however, the soul of the one who remains behind on earth begins to light up, to exist for the dead.

Do not object by saying that it is an injustice that people who have no spiritual thoughts here on earth, and perhaps it is not even their fault, should remain invisible to the dead. If the world were arranged otherwise, man would never seek to strive for perfection. Man has to learn by what he foregoes. Such a soul, as a result of the pain and loneliness it suffers during life between death and rebirth, is given the impulse to receive spiritual thoughts. From this aspect we see that spiritual science is like a language by means of which the living and the dead may understand one another, and can be present for and perceptible to each other.

Spiritual science has yet another mission in connection with bridging the abyss between the living and the dead. When human souls go through the gate of death they enter a realm where the connection with life on earth is maintained by the recollection of what has happened there. I am not repeating what can be found in my written works. What I am now saying is intended as a supplement. For a long period after death man re-experiences what has happened on earth and has to rid himself of the longing for his physical body. During this time he learns to live as a soul-spirit being. Let us vividly imagine how this appears to supersensible perception. To begin with, the soul has a connection with itself. One sees one's own inner life that has run its course in thoughts, in mental representations, etc. One recalls the relationships one has had with his fellow men.

If one seeks to look down upon it, the earth offers a special aspect. One has the urge to look down. The urge to remember the earth accompanies one throughout the whole of life between death and a new birth. As long as man is called to journey from life to life the consciousness remains that he is destined for the earth, that he must return again and again to the earth if he would develop himself rightly. We can see this with the dead because if he were to lose completely the thoughts that link him to the earth, he would also lose the thought of his own ego. Then he would no longer be aware that he is, and this would result in the most dreadful feeling of anguish. Man must not lose his connection with the earth. The earth must not escape his mental representation, so to speak. In general, too, the earth cannot completely disappear from him. It is only in our period of the materialistic deluge, during which the spiritual revelation has to come so that the link between the living and the dead may be maintained, that souls having no connection with people who have spiritual thoughts and feelings on earth find it difficult to look back.

It is important for the dead that those with whom they were connected on earth carry every evening thoughts of the spiritual world with them into sleep. The more thoughts about the spiritual world we carry with us into sleep, the greater the service we perform for those we have known on earth who have died before us. It is difficult to speak of these connections because our words are taken from the physical plane. In the spiritual world what we bring with us as spiritual thoughts in sleep is the substance by means of which, in a certain sense, the dead can live. One who dies and has no one on earth who carries spiritual thoughts with him in sleep is famished and may be compared to one banished to a barren island on earth. The dead person who cannot find a soul in whom spiritual feelings dwell experiences himself as if in a desert void of everything that is needed to sustain life. In view of this, one cannot stress too much the earnestness with which thoughts of spiritual science should be taken in a period like our own, when world-conceptions that are alien to the spirit gain the upper hand more and more.

It was different in past times when an evening prayer was said before going to sleep and its after-effects accompanied one. Today it is more likely than not that a person falls asleep after a meal or some other form of enjoyment without a thought devoted to the supersensible. In this way we rob the dead of their spiritual nourishment. Such insight should lead to the practice, proven to be effective by many of our friends, that I would like to term, *the reading to the dead.* To read to the dead is of untold significance.

Let us assume that two people lived side by side here on earth. The one finds his way to spiritual science out of a deep, heartfelt impulse, the other is increasingly repelled by it. In such a case little is achieved in attempting to bring the person to a spiritual concept of the world during life. In fact, one's endeavors in this direction may indeed cause the other to hate it all the more. Now when such a person dies we have the possibility of helping him all the more.

What lives in our soul is exceedingly complex and the area bounded by our consciousness is only a small part of the total content of our soul life. Man does not know much of what lives in his soul and often something is present that he takes for the opposite of what is actually there. Thus it can happen that a person comes to hate spiritual science. He becomes aware of this with his consciousness. In the depths of his soul, however, this can reveal itself as an all the more profound longing for spiritual science. When we have gone through the gate of death we experience the depths of our soul existence that come to the surface. When we meet the dead we have known on earth, they often show themselves to be different from what they were on earth. A person who has hated spiritual science with his normal consciousness but longed for it in the depths of his soul without being aware of it will often display this longing powerfully after death. We can help him by taking a book with a spiritual-scientific content, forming a vivid inner picture of the one who has died, and reading to him as we would to a living person, not with a loud voice, but softly. The dead can understand this. Naturally, those who have made a contact with spiritual science during their lifetime understand it all the more readily. We should not fail to read to the dead or converse with them in thought. I would like to draw attention to a practical matter, namely, that for a number of years after death, for a period of some three to five years, a person can understand the language he has spoken on earth. This gradually wanes, but he preserves an understanding of spiritual thoughts. Then we can also read to the dead in a language that he did not understand on earth but that we have ourselves mastered. In this way we can perform the greatest service to the dead.

It is particularly in such realms that one realized the full significance of spiritual science because it bridges the gulf between the living and the dead. We can imagine that if we succeed in spreading spiritual science on earth in ever wider circles, more and more souls will become conscious of a communion with the dead.

Thus for a period after death man is still directly connected with the earth. Then he has to grow into and become a citizen of the spiritual world. This requires preparation.

He first must possess a sensitivity and understanding for the spiritual world. Spiritual investigation observes a considerable difference after death between souls who have cultivated moral feelings and inclinations on earth and those who have failed to do so. A person who has not developed moral feelings on earth becomes a hermit after death. He will be unable to find his way both to other human beings and to the higher hierarchies. Consciousness is not extinguished then, and what awaits man is a sense of utter loneliness. From a certain period called the Mercury period onward man gains the possibility of living together with other beings by virtue of his moral life. We may say therefore that the way a person lives on earth determines his existence in the Mercury sphere, determines whether he experiences a dreadful hermit-like existence or establishes contact with other human souls or the beings of the higher hierarchies.

This is followed by another period during which man must be differently prepared if he does not again condemn himself to loneliness. Loneliness comes to pass if he has not developed any religious feelings here on earth. This period is called the Venus period. There a person who has failed to develop religious feelings experiences himself as blind and dead in relation to everything that surrounds him.

In a subsequent period, so as not to remain insensitive toward the beings of the higher world, a preparation in the complete appreciation of all religions is necessary. That is the Sun period. We prepare for it here on earth by an understanding for all that is human, and for the different religious denominations. In former times in the Sun period it sufficed for one man to belong to the Brahma religion, for another to that of Lao-Tse, and so forth. Today, however, because times have changed men stand opposite one another through their religious creeds and therefore the Sun period cannot be rightly experienced. For this a spiritual sensitivity is needed.

In the Sun period, which man has to traverse between death and a new birth, it is as if one entered into a world where one found a particular place empty or filled, depending on one's preparation. We do not find the place empty if we understand the Mystery of Golgotha. The Christ impulse affords the possibility of understanding every human experience. Christianity is a general religion, valid for all people. Christianity is not limited to a particular folk, race or nationality, as is the case with Hinduism and other national religions. Had the people of middle Europe preserved their old folk religion, we would still today find a Wotan cult, a Thor cult, and so on. But the European people have accepted the Christian creed. One is not a Christian in the true sense because one adheres to one or the other Christian dogma, however, but because one knows that Christ died for the whole of humanity. Only gradually will people learn to live truly as Christians.

In our time most Europeans in India pay mere lip service to their own belief. The attitude that one should develop is that wherever we meet a human being in the face of the earth the Christ impulse can be found. The Hindu will not believe that his god dwells in every man. The Christian knows that Christ lives in every human being. Spiritual science will reveal that the true core of all religions is contained in a rightly understood Christianity, and that every religion, inasmuch as it becomes conscious of its essential kernel, leads to the Mystery of Golgotha.

In considering other initiates or religious founders it is

evident that they seek to reveal certain things out of the higher worlds because they have gone through a process of initiation. We do not understand the Christ correctly if we do not clearly see that the Christ has not gone through one or the other form of initiation on earth. He was initiated by virtue of the fact that He was there and united everything within Himself.

When the seer looks at the life of the Buddha and then follows it through in the spiritual world, he realizes more clearly the true nature of the Buddha. This is not so with the life of Christ. The Christ life is such that one must first establish a connection with it on earth in order to understand it in the spiritual world. If one does not gain such a connection and one is nevertheless initiated, one can behold many things, but one cannot see the Christ if one has not first gained a connection with Him on earth.

That is why so few people understand the Mystery of Golgotha. The Christ is a Being who is of equal importance for the most primitive human being and for the highest initiate. The most primitive soul can find a relationship to Christ, and the initiate must also find it. One learns to know many things when one enters into the spiritual world. There is only one thing that does not exist there, one thing that cannot be learned there and that is death. Death exists only in the physical world. In the spiritual world there is transformation but not death. Therefore, all the spiritual beings who never descend to the earth and only dwell in spiritual realms do not go through death.

Christ has become the companion of man on earth and the event of Golgotha, if one understands it as the unique death of a god, is what prevents us from confronting emptiness in the Sun period. The other initiates are human beings who through a number of incarnations have developed themselves in a special way. Christ had never been on the earth before His advent but dwelt in realms where there is no death. He is the only one among the gods who has learned to know death. Therefore, in order to become acquainted with the Christ one has to understand His death, and because this is essential the Mystery of Golgotha can be understood only on earth where death exists. We do not experience the Christ in higher worlds if we have not gained a relationship to Him on earth. We find His place empty during the Sun period. If, however, we are able to take the Christ impulse with us, then the throne in the Sun is not empty. Then we find the Christ consciously.

During our present phase of human evolution it is important that we should find the Christ in the spiritual world at this stage and recognize Him. Why? In the Sun period we have gradually entered a realm in which we are dependent on spiritual light. Previously, before the Sun period, we still experienced the after-effects of the earth, the after-effects of what we have been personally, including our moral and religious feelings. Now we require more than these. Now we require the faculty to see what is in the spiritual world, but this cannot be prepared for on earth. We have to journey through realms of forces of which we cannot know anything here on earth.

As he enters into life through birth, man has not as yet got a developed brain. He first must form it in accordance with the achievements of previous earth lives. For if one needs a particular faculty it is not sufficient that one has acquired it. One also has to know how the requisite physical organ has to be formed.

There exists an important but dangerous leader. Here on

earth he remains unconscious, but from the Sun period onward he is necessary. The leader is Lucifer. We would wander in darkness if Lucifer were not to approach us. However, we can only walk beside him if we are guided by the Christ. Together they lead man after the Sun period in subsequent forms of life, that is, through the Mars, Jupiter and Saturn periods. During the times following the Sun period, man is brought together with forces that he requires for his next incarnation. It is sheer nonsense to believe as materialistic science does that the physical body is inherited. Today science cannot see its error but spiritual truths will be acknowledged in the future and the fallacy, too, will be recognized. For nothing can be inherited apart from the basic structure of the brain and the spinal cord, that is, everything that is contained within and bounded by the hard skull cap and the vertebrae of the spinal column. Everything else is conditioned by forces from the macrocosmos. If man were only given what he inherits he would be a totally inhuman lump, so to speak. The inherited part has to be worked through by what man brings with him out of the spiritual world.

Why do I use the terms Mercury, Venus, Sun, Mars, Jupiter and Saturn for the periods after death? When man has gone through the gate of death he expands more and more. In fact, life after death is such that one knows oneself to be spread out over a vast space. This expansion goes so far that one finally occupies the space bounded by the orbit of the moon. Then one grows out to the orbit of Mercury in the occult sense, then out to the orbits of Venus, Sun and Mars. One grows out into the vast celestial spaces. But the spatial togetherness of the many human souls is not significant. When you permeate the whole of the Venus sphere this is also the case for the others, but it does not mean that because of this you are aware of them. Even if one knows that one is not alone, one can still feel lonely.

Finally one expands into the universe in a sphere circumscribed by the orbit of Saturn and beyond. As one grows in this way one gathers the forces needed to build up the next incarnation. Then one returns. One becomes ever smaller until one unites oneself again with the earth.

Between death and rebirth man expands into the whole cosmos and however strange it may appear, when we return to the earth we bring all the forces of the solar system with us into life and unite them with what is inherited out of the physical substances. By means of the cosmic forces we build up our physical body and our brain. Here between birth and death we dwell within the narrow confines of our physical body. After death we live, expanded, into the entire solar macrocosm.

The one person has a deep moral sense, the other less so. The one who on earth had a deep moral sense goes through the spiritual world in such a way that he can experience everything as a sociable being. The power for this flows from the starry realms. Another who is not thus prepared is unable to make any connections and because he did not bring any spiritualized forces with him, he also is unable to receive any moral predispositions. He will journey alone through the various spheres. Such spiritual knowledge throws significant light on everything that a man is and on his relationship to the world.

Kant uttered the saying, "There are two things that fill my mind with an ever new and increasing sense of wonder and devotion: The starry heavens above me and the moral law within me." He thereby expressed something significant.

Spiritual science reveals that both are one and the same. What we experience between death and rebirth we bring with us as moral law. We carry the starry heavens through which we journey between death and a new birth into our earthly life where it must become moral law.

Thus spiritual science brings us insight into the magnitude of the human soul and the idea of human responsibility.

INTERCOURSE WITH THE DEAD

Düsseldorf, April 27, 1913

XV

INTERCOURSE WITH THE DEAD

Düsseldorf, April 27, 1913

THE CONNECTION between life and death is mostly misunderstood. In theosophical writings one often finds the remark that man's soul and spirit-being could completely disappear. It is stated, for example, that through a certain amount of evil with which the soul burdens itself the human soul could disappear in the course of evolution. It is further emphasized that black magicians who have wrought much evil will encounter this fate.

Those who have already shared in our aims for a longer period will know that I have always opposed such statements. Above all, we must hold fast to the fact that what we term death on the physical plane has no meaning in the supersensible world. This is even the case for the region of the supersensible that immediately borders upon our world. I will deal with this matter from a certain aspect.

The science that deals with the physical world has arrived at a number of laws and connections within the physical realm. These laws when applied to the outer phenomena of nature can only tell us something about the structure of external sense perceptible reality. A flower, for example, investigated by means of natural science, will tell us certain facts about the physical and chemical laws operating

281

within the plant, but life itself always eludes such scientific observation. It is, of course, true that in recent times a few specially imaginative scientists have constructed a body of hypotheses to explain how plant life arises from mere dead substances. Such attempts are rapidly recognized as erroneous because in science it remains merely an ideal to grasp the reality of life. Ever more knowledge is accumulated about chemical laws and so forth, but nothing about life itself. The investigation of life is for the natural scientific method a mere ideal because it is something that streams out of the supersensible realm into the physical world and within this world its laws cannot be fathomed.

Now, similarly, what is true for life in the physical world obtains for death in the supersensible world, except that there it is a question of the will. In the supersensible world an act of will, a will impulse, can never lead to what we know on earth as death. At most, a longing for death may arise in the supersensible world but never death itself. Death does not exist in the realms beyond the physical. This fact is particularly moving for the human soul when it realizes that all the beings of the hierarchies can never know death. It can only be experienced on earth.

Just as the biblical saying is justified that tells that the angels conceal their countenances from beholding the mysteries of physical birth, so it is also correct to say that they hide their faces from beholding the mysteries of death. That being whom we know as the One Who has given the mightiest impulse to earth evolution, the Christ Being, is the only being in divine realms Who learned to know death. All other divine-spiritual beings do not know death. They only know it as a transformation from one form into another.

The Christ had to descend to the earth in order to experience death. Christ is the only being among all the supersensible beings above man who has become acquainted with death through his own experience. As I indicated, if one views the problem relating to the death experience in connection with the Christ, it is found to be deeply stirring.

Now it is literally true that man, when he has crossed the portal of death, lives in that supersensible world in which there is no death. He can enter these realms but he cannot annihilate himself because he is received into worlds where there can be no destruction.

There is something of a similar nature to death in the supersensible world, yet it is quite different from death as we know it. One would have to call it in human language, loneliness. Death can never mean the annihilation of something that takes place in the supersensible worlds, but loneliness does arise. Loneliness in the supersensible world is comparable to death here. It is not destruction but it is far more intense than loneliness as we know it on earth. It takes the form of looking back upon one's own being. One only knows what this fully means when it happens, that is, to know nothing except to know about oneself.

Let us take as an example a person who developed on earth what one may call little sympathy for his fellow men, a person who has lived essentially for himself. Such a being encounters difficulties after death, especially in getting to know other human souls. Such a person can live together with others in the supersensible world without being in the least aware of their existence. He is filled only with his own soul content. He is aware only of what lives within himself.

It may happen that a person who has avoided any form

of human love on earth because of an exaggerated sense of egoism is only able to live in the memory of his last earthly existence when he has gone through the gate of death. He is unable to gain any new experiences because he neither knows nor can enter into contact with any being. He is completely dependent on himself because as human beings on earth we do indeed prepare a particular world for ourselves after death.

Here on earth man does not truly know himself. Science teaches us only what we are when we are no longer because it only knows the corpse. The brain thinks but it cannot think itself. We see a portion of ourselves, a larger portion when we look in the mirror, but that is only the outer aspect. On earth man does not live in himself. He lives together with the surrounding world that impinges upon his senses. Through ourselves, through all that we experience here, we prepare to expand into the macrocosmos, to become a macrocosmos, to become all we see around us on earth.

Here we see the moon. After death we expand in such a way that we become the moon, just as on earth we are our brain. We expand into Saturn so that we become Saturn, just as we are now our spleen. Man becomes a macrocosmic being. When the soul has departed from the body it expands into the entirety of the planetary system so that all souls simultaneously dwell within the same spatial area. They interpenetrate one another but without being aware of it. Spiritual connections only determine whether we know about one another or not. A preparation is made during our life on earth to expand into the whole of the universe that we behold here in its physical reflection. But what in fact is our world?

Just as now we are surrounded by mountains, rivers,

trees, animals and minerals, so then we live in the universe. The universe becomes our organism. These are our organs and that world is we, ourselves. We behold ourselves from the surroundings. This process begins in the ether body immediately after death. We then behold the tableau of our life.

If it were not for the fact that a man makes connections with other human beings and, as will happen more and more frequently through spiritual science, with beings of the higher hierarchies, he would have no occupation after death apart from continuously beholding himself. This is not meant trivially because it is truly a shattering fact that to behold only oneself through a number of centuries is not a particularly enviable prospect. We have then become a world for ourselves, but it is the connections that we have made on earth that open wider vistas for the self after death. Earthly life is there so that we develop connections and relationships that can be continued after death. Everything that makes us into sociable beings after death must be prepared on earth. Fear of loneliness is the torment that man experiences in the spiritual world. This fear befalls us again and again because we traverse a number of stages between death and rebirth. Even if we experience a measure of sociability at one stage, we may fall into loneliness during the next.

The first period after death is such that we can only establish a good connection with souls who have remained on the earth or with those who have died about the same time as ourselves. Here the closest connections continue to be effective beyond death. Much can be done by the so-called living who have remained on the earth. Because one has a connection with the departed soul he can inform him of his own knowledge of the spiritual world acquired on the earth. This is possible above all by reading to the dead.

We can perform the greatest service to a dead person by forming a picture of him in our soul and softly reading a work of spiritual science to him, instructing him as it were. We can also convey to the departed thoughts we have made our own, always vividly picturing the one who has passed on as we do so. We should not be miserly in this respect. This enables us to bridge the abyss that separates us from the dead. It is not only in extreme cases that we can help the dead in this way. No, it is true in every case. It provides a comforting feeling that can alleviate the sorrow that is experienced when a person whom one has loved passes on.

The deeper we enter into the supersensible world, the less do particular relationships obtain. We still find individual relationships in the astral world but the higher we ascend, the more we find that what weaves between separate beings no longer continues. Now there are beings everywhere. The relationships among them are of a soul nature. We need these also in order not to be lonely. It is, however, the mission of the earth that we make contacts from man to man because otherwise we remain solitary in the spiritual world.

For the first phases after death our world consists of the relationships, the friendships that we formed with fellow human beings on earth and that now continue. For instance, if the matter is investigated with supersensible perception, one finds the departed soul in the vicinity of a person whom it can follow on earth. Many people in our time live with those who have died recently or at some earlier period. One also sees how many come together with a number of their ancestors to whom they were related by blood.

The seer often comes upon the fact that the departed soul links itself to ancestors that have died centuries ago but this only lasts for a certain period of time. The person would again feel exceedingly lonely if other connections did not exist which, though far off, yet prepare the person to be sociable in the spiritual world. Within our movement we have found a fundamental principle that stems from a cosmic task that has been entrusted to us. It is to form relationships among human beings in the most varied ways. Anthroposophy is therefore not only cultivated by giving lectures. Within the Anthroposophical Society we seek to bring people together so that personal relationships may also form themselves. These connections have their validity also for the supersensible world inasmuch as a person who belongs to a particular stream in the Society creates connections for the realm beyond the physical.

The time comes, however, when more general connections are necessary. A phase approaches when souls who have gone through the gate of death without any moral soul disposition, without moral concepts, that is, souls who have rejected a moral disposition of soul during their earthly life, feel lonely. People who are endowed with a moral soul disposition are simply of greater value here on earth than people lacking in morality. A moral human being is of greater worth for the whole of humanity in the same way that a sound healthy stomach is more valuable to the whole man than a sick one.

It is not easy to put one's finger on where the value of the moral human being lies for the whole of humanity, and on the harm created by an immoral person, but you will understand what I mean when I put it as follows. A person devoid of a moral soul disposition is a sick member of humanity. This means that through this immoral soul disposition he alienates himself increasingly from other people. To be moral also means to acknowledge that one has a relationship to all men. That is why love of all humanity is self-evident to all moral people. Immoral people feel lonely at a certain phase after death owing to their lack of morality. The torments of loneliness at this stage can only be dispelled by the moral disposition of our soul.

So if we investigate the lives of human beings spread out in the macrocosmos after death, we see that the immoral individuals are in fact lonely while the moral individuals find a rapport with others of like moral ideas. Here on earth men are grouped in accordance with nationality or in some other way. Between death and rebirth people also group themselves, but according to the moral concepts and soul dispositions they have in common.

This is followed by a phase of development such that even those who are endowed with a moral disposition of soul feel lonely if they lack religious concepts. A religious turn of mind is the preparation for sociability at a particular stage of life between death and rebirth. Here we also discover that those people who are unable to enter into religious feelings and connections are condemned to loneliness. We find people of like religious confessions grouped together.

This is followed by a period when it is no longer sufficient to have lived within a religious community. A phase draws near when one can again feel loneliness. This period is a particularly important one between death and rebirth. Either we feel alone even though we experienced togetherness with those of like religious confession, or we are able to bring understanding to every human soul in its essential character. For this communion we can only prepare by gaining an understanding of all religious confessions. Prior to the Mystery of Golgotha this was not necessary because the experiences in the spiritual world were different then. Now it has become essential, and the correct understanding of Christianity is a preparatory step toward it. We cannot encounter what constitutes the essential being of Christianity in other religious creeds. It is not correct to place Christianity next to other religious creeds. Indeed, perhaps certain Christian confessions are narrow-minded. Nevertheless, Christianity rightly understood bears within it the impulse to grasp all religious creeds and tendencies.

How has the Westerner grasped Christianity? Consider Hinduism. Only those belonging to the Hindu race can be adherents of it. If a racial religion were prevalent in Europe, for instance, we would still have a Wotan cult today that would be the equivalent of an occidental racial religion. But the West has accepted a confession that did not arise out of its own folk-substance. It came from the East. Something was accepted that could only work through its spiritual content. The Christ impulse cannot be sucked up into a racial or folk religion. Actually, the folk among whom the Christ appeared did not acknowledge Him. That is the remarkable fact about Christianity. It contains the seed enabling it to become the universal religion.

One need not take an intolerant attitude toward other religions. The mission of Christianity does not consist in bringing dogma to people. Naturally the Buddhist smiles at a confession that does not even contain the idea of reincarnation. Such a confession must appear to him as erroneous. Christianity rightly understood, however, presupposes that every man is a Christian in his inner being. If you go to a Hindu and say to him, "You are a Hindu and I am a Christian," it will be seen that you have not understood Christianity. Christianity has been truly understood only if you can say of the Hindu, "Inwardly this Hindu is as good a Christian as I am. He has as yet only had the opportunity to become acquainted with a preparatory confession. I must endeavor to show him where his religion and mine correspond." The best thing would be for Christians to teach Hinduism to the Hindus and then attempt to take Hinduism a stage further so that the Hindu could gain a point of contact with the general stream of evolution. We understand Christianity only if we look upon each individual as a Christian in the depth of his heart. Only then is Christianity the religion that transcends race, color and social position. That is Christianity.

We enter a new age. Christianity can no longer work in the way it did over the last centuries. It is the task of anthroposophy to bring about the new understanding of Christianity that is needed. In this connection the anthroposophical view of the world is an instrument of Christianity. Among the religions of the earth, Christianity has appeared last. New religions cannot be founded anymore. Such foundations belong to the past. They followed one another and brought forth Christianity as the last flower. Today the task is to form and apply the impulses of Christianity. That is why in our spiritual scientific movement we endeavor to consider all the religions of the world more consciously than heretofore, and in loving participation. In this way we also prepare ourselves for the period between death and rebirth when we experience loneliness if we cannot perceive and have no access to other souls within this realm.

If on earth we misunderstand Hinduism, we might only sense the presence of a Hindu in the world beyond but remain unable to gain any contact with him.

You see, this is the phase during life between death and rebirth when we have also expanded our astral body so far as to become Sun inhabitants. We enter into the Sun realm. We do in fact expand into the entire macrocosmos, and reach the Sun Being when we need the capacity for brotherly love. The encounter with the Sun is shown by the following. Firstly, we lose the possibility of having understanding for all human beings unless we have gained a connection to the words, "Wherever two are gathered in My Name, there I am in the midst of them." Christ did not mean wherever two Hindus or one Hindu and one Christian are gathered together, there He is in the midst of them, but wherever two are gathered who have a genuine understanding for His impulse, there He is in the midst of them.

This Being was within the Sun sphere until a particular period. His throne was also there. Then He united Himself with the earth. Therefore we must experience the Christ impulse here on earth and thus also carry it upwards into the spiritual world. For if we arrive in the Sun sphere without the Christ impulse we are faced with an unintelligible entry in the Akasha Chronicle. Since the Christ has united Himself with the earth, we have to gain an understanding on earth for the Christ. We have to bring a Christ understanding with us because otherwise the Christ cannot be found after death. As we approach the Sun sphere we understand the entry in the Akasha Chronicle if we have gained an understanding for the Christ on earth. For He left this behind in the Sun sphere. That is the important factor —that the understanding of the Christ must be stimulated on the earth. Then it also can be preserved in higher worlds. Things only become clear if they can be viewed in a certain configuration.

Some theosophical circles are unable to realize that the Christ impulse stands as a fulcrum at the center of earth evolution, the point from which the ascending curve begins. To maintain that Christ can appear repeatedly on earth is like saying that the beam of a balance must be supported at two points. But with such scales one cannot weigh. A conviction of this sort is as senseless in relation to the physical world as the statement made by certain occultists that Christ goes through repeated earth lives. One has gained an understanding of the Christ impulse only if one is able to grasp that the Christ is the only god who has gone through death and hence first had to descend to the earth.

For one who has gained an understanding of the Christ down here, the throne in the Sun will not be empty. This also enables him to recognize the nature of a particular encounter that occurs at this stage. The human being meets Lucifer, not as the tempter but as a legitimate power who has to travel by his side if he is to progress in his journey. Qualities of the same nature in the wrong sphere have a destructive effect. The workings of Lucifer in the physical world are evil, but after death, from the Sun sphere onwards, man needs Lucifer as a companion. He must meet Lucifer, and he has to continue his further journey between Lucifer and Christ. Christ preserves his soul nature with the total assets that his soul has accumulated in previous incarnations. It is the task of the luciferic power to assist man so that he may also learn to apply the forces of the other hierarchical beings in the right manner for his next incarnation.

Irrespective of when the stage that has just been described occurs, man is faced with the necessity of determining what part of the globe and in which country he is to reincarnate. This has to be determined at the mid-point between death and rebirth. In fact, the first thing that must be determined is the location and the country where the soul is to reincarnate.

On earth man prepares for this stage inasmuch as he acquires a connection with the supersensible world, but he needs Lucifer's support. He now receives from beings of the higher hierarchies forces that guide him to a certain place at a certain time.

Let us consider an outstanding example. Luther's appearance at a specific moment had to be prepared from the ninth century onward. Already at that time forces had to be directed in the appropriate people. Lucifer has to cooperate to this end so that the time and place of our reembodiment may be determined. Through the fact that an individual harbors Christ in his soul, what he has gained by dint of effort is preserved. But man is not yet sufficiently mature to know where his karma can best be worked out and for this, Lucifer's assistance is needed.

A further period of time elapses and then a major matter has to be decided that involves a deeply stirring activity. By means of our everyday language it can only be described as follows. The question now has to be resolved as to how the parents of the soul that is to incarnate at a certain time and place are to be endowed with their own characteristics so as to give birth to *that* particular being. All this has to be determined long in advance. But this means that the higher hierarchies, supported again by Lucifer, must work in a preparatory way through the whole genealogical stream long before the incarnation of the particular individual. In Luther's case his ancestors had to be determined as early as the tenth and eleventh centuries so that he might have the right parents.

Science believes that a person takes on the characteristics of his ancestors. Actually he influences the characteristics of his ancestors from the supersensible world. In a certain sense we ourselves are responsible for the way our great-great-great-grandparents were. Obviously, we cannot influence all their characteristics and yet, among others, those must be present that we ourselves later require. What one inherits from one's ancestors one first has oneself instilled into them.

First the time and place of birth are determined; then the ancestry is chosen. Fundamentally, what is called a child's love for his parents is the emergence of a union with a stream in which he has worked for centuries from the supersensible world. At the moment of conception the individual receives the forces that cooperate in the formation of his own body, namely, of the head and the general bodily form. We must so picture these forces that from then onwards they are mainly active in the deeper structure of the head, less in the hands and feet, less also in the trunk, but going from the head towards the trunk. We lay the foundation for this, and after birth we continue to shape it. First everything is woven into the astral body. The shape of the head is prefigured astrally. This goes so far that actually only at the final stage is the shape of the cranium incorporated into the astral prototype that then unites with the bodily formation. The shape of the head is individual, and the shape of the brain is chiseled out at the last stage. Then what we receive through the hereditary stream is able to unite with what we bring with us out of the supersensible world. Picture what comes from the supersensible world as the chalice. The water that fills it is provided by the hereditary substance. The pure stream of heredity provides only the characteristics of the part of our bodily constitution that is more independent from the system of blood and nerves. Whether we have big and strong or weak and fine bones depends more on heredity than on the forces we receive from the preparatory spiritual powers.

The individuality that is to be born at a particular time and place in order to work out his karma may be the child of parents with strong bones or blond hair, and so forth. This is made possible by the hereditary stream. If the theories of physical heredity were correct, men would appear with deformed nervous systems and a mere indication of hands and feet.

Only supersensible insight is able to lead to matters that are truly meaningful. Let me relate an actual instance. I met a hydrocephalic child who was different in many respects from the rest of his family. Why was he a hydrocephalic? Because the council of higher powers together with Lucifer had decreed that that particular individuality should be born in a particular place and his parents were the best available for him. But he was unable to work rightly into the ancestral line so he could create what would result in the appropriate substance in order that his head might harden in the right way. Only during his lifetime would he be able to adapt his brain to its general structure. Such an individuality did not find the right conditions enabling him to influence his ancestry so that his head could harden in the appropriate way.

These matters are of considerable importance and also show the technique that has to be adopted in order to go out into the world at large. When the time comes in which such questions will be rightly understood by science, the workings of the higher worlds, also, will be felt.

If we continue our journey with Lucifer *and* Christ we acquire the right relationship to the progressive stream in evolution.

In conclusion, during life after death one first has to overcome the dangers of loneliness by means of one's relationships to other human beings, by means of moral and religious connections. Then one fashions the new man that is to incarnate in the future. One now has a task that involves facing oneself instead of facing the world.

If a human being goes through the stages during which he could have been sociable but was condemned to loneliness, a longing arises in him after death. He longs for a condition of unconsciousness. But consciousness is not lost; one merely becomes lonely. In the higher worlds matter no longer exists. Everything there is a question of consciousness. This is true of souls who lack a connection to other souls. Death does not exist in the world beyond.

As here we live rhythmically between waking and sleeping, so in the other world life alternates between withdrawal into ourselves and sociable intercourse with other souls. As I have described above, our life in the higher worlds depends on how we have prepared ourselves here on earth.

* * *

Dr. Steiner gave the following answer to the question of whether one also could read to children who have died at birth or in early childhood.

One is a child only here on earth. Supersensible vision frequently reveals that a person who dies at an early age is less childlike in the spiritual world than many who cross the portal of death at eighty. The same criterion therefore cannot be applied.

On a previous occasion I have spoken of how we are to understand occultly the painting known as "The School of Athens." Recently I came to know an individuality who died an early death. My connection with him enabled me to become aware of Raphael's original intention in relation to this painting. This being explained that on the left near the group in the foreground a part had been painted over. It is the spot where something is being written down. Today we find there a mathematical formula. Originally there was a gospel passage. So you see that a "child" can be a highly evolved individuality able to guide one to things that can be discovered only with great difficulty.

I would say therefore that one also can practice reading to children who have died young.

LIFE AFTER DEATH

Strasbourg, May 13, 1913

XVI

LIFE AFTER DEATH

Strasbourg, May 13, 1913

WE ENCOUNTER the full significance and the tasks of spiritual science when we consider the period of life between death and a new birth. There are many people, particularly in our materialistic age, who ask why they should concern themselves with life between death and rebirth or, if the idea of repeated earth lives is rejected, with an existence after death, since they surely can wait and see what happens after death when the time comes! This is said by people today who have not quite lost the feeling for the spiritual world but who are not yet equipped with sufficient soul-powers to acquire concepts and feelings about the supersensible. They add that if they perform their duty here on earth, they shall experience in the appropriate way what awaits them after death.

Now a genuine connection with life between death and rebirth brings out clearly the fallacy of such a view and how important it is during earthly existence to have formed an idea of the conditions of life after death.

It is exceedingly difficult to speak about life after death in words borrowed from everyday language since the language we know is adapted to life between birth and death and refers to the objects of this world. Therefore, we can usually only indicate what happens between death and a new birth, which is so radically different in nature from anything that can be experienced here. We must imagine that everything we perceive here in the physical world to which we belong cannot be our world after death because we lack the physical-sensory organs. The intellect, which is bound to the brain, also ceases to function after death. We can only tentatively endeavor to give a picture of the life that is so completely different from our existence here on earth. In a certain sense, everyday words can only be used as analogies. Spiritual science, however, also teaches us to relate words to spiritual reality and conveys by means of words an understanding of the supersensible world.

In the physical world, by the physical in man we mean that which is enclosed within his skin, the rest is known as his surroundings, what we experience depends on the functions of our sense organs but also on the heart, lungs and so forth. All this vanishes in the course of our journey between death and a new birth. During earthly existence our soul-spiritual being is embedded in our physical body, and it lives on the activity of our organs. After death the part that leaves the physical and etheric bodies grows ever larger, and a time comes when what is otherwise contained within the boundary of the skin expands so far as to fill the whole circumference of the orbit of the Moon. The soul-spirit gradually grows right up to the Mercury and Venus spheres, and farther to the Mars, Jupiter and Saturn spheres, and even beyond into the universe. Later it contracts again and unites itself as a tiny spirit-germ with the stream of heredity that prepares its physical body through father and mother. This description agrees with what has been written in *Theosophy*. The Spirit Land begins in the Mars sphere.

From the above it can be deduced that having gone through the gate of death we all find ourselves within the same cosmic space. After death we do in a sense interpenetrate one another, yet all the dead are not together because togetherness after death depends upon something quite other than what it depends upon on earth. In the spiritual world we may be spatially united but we can only really be together with another individual if we have a spiritual connection with him.

Let us take the extreme case of a person who, while on earth, has utterly denied the spirit both in his thoughts and in his feelings. There are many theoretical materialists who deny the spirit and who nevertheless are in some way through their feelings connected with the spiritual world. In reality there are hardly any people who totally deny the spiritual world so that the fearful circumstances I am about to describe never quite come into effect. Let us assume that two such persons die who knew one another well on earth. After death they will dwell within the same space but will be completely unaware of one another because after death a feeling for the spirit corresponds, let us say, to what here are our eyes. Without eyes, no light; without a feeling for the spiritual, no perception of the supersensible world.

But an even more terrible fate than not being able to perceive the spiritual world is in store for such people. Because souls who go through the gate of death are of a spiritual nature, materialistic souls cannot even perceive them. A yawning chasm opens up around such souls. In fact, one may ask, "What does such a soul perceive after death?" Not even himself as he is after death because he lacks a clear consciousness of self. The following will show us what remains for him.

Here on the earth we are situated at a point on the earth's surface. Our organs are within us, whereas the starry heavens are outside. The opposite is the case after death. Then man grows to a cosmic dimension. When he has expanded up to the Moon sphere, the spiritual that belongs to the Moon becomes an organ within him. It becomes after death what the brain is for us on earth as physical human beings. Each planetary body becomes an organ for us after death inasmuch as we have expanded to its orbit. The Sun becomes a heart for us. As here we bear the physical heart within our body, so there we carry the spiritual part of the Sun within us. There is only one difference. We are perfect physical human beings when, after the embryonic evolution, all the organs have formed; they are simultaneously present. After death we acquire these organs little by little, one after another. We are then in this respect, considered externally, quite similar to a plant-like being that also forms its organs successively. We may, for example, compare the organ we receive on Mars with the lungs and the larynx.

After death we grow into that of which the physical part has been discarded, and the spiritual part of the cosmic organ is now inside us. What is then our external world? What at present is our inner world, what we have experienced by means of our organs that make us into physical, earthly beings, and what we have done by means of these organs.

Let us again take the extreme case of the person who has made no connection whatsoever to the spiritual world. After death his outer world consists of what he has been able to experience by means of his physical organs. For such a radical atheist the world after death is totally devoid of human souls and he is forced to look back on his earthly life, on what was *his* world, on what he encompassed with his deeds and experiences. That is his external world. It consists of nothing apart from the memories that remain of his life between birth and death, and that is not sufficient for what man requires for his life between death and rebirth. In fact, when man dwells outside his skin, his earthly existence looks quite different.

For example, on earth we are connected with a person towards whom we feel antipathy, with whom we have quarrelled and whom we have insulted and caused pain. We are emotionally involved with him and we would not behave in this way unless in a certain sense we found such behaviour gratifying. One is perhaps filled with remorse, and then again one forgets about it.

After death we again meet this person but now we feel the opposite of the satisfaction previously experienced. One senses that if one had not acted in this way, one would have been a more perfect human being; one's soul is wanting in this respect. This shortcoming now remains in the soul until the deed can be adjusted. We do not behold the deed as much as the failing in our soul, which must be removed. We experience this as an inner force that leads us to find an opportunity to wipe away the deed.

In the case of an anti-spiritual soul something else must be added, because he feels he is severed from the soul he has dealt with unjustly, and he must wait until he meets him again in order to remove the stain. A feeling for the necessity of karma is the result of looking back at the previous earth life. The tableau in the Akasha Chronicle of the other soul stands before us in admonition. Then we dwell merely among such pictures in the Akasha Chronicle.

Such extreme cases do not actually exist. The initiate who enters into contact with the soul of a dead person can have the following experience. He finds a soul with whom he is acquainted and who has gone out of a male body through the portal of death leaving behind him wife and children. This soul tells him, "I have left behind my wife and my children with whom I lived. Now I have only the images of what we experienced together. My family is on the earth, but I cannot see them. I feel separated from them. Perhaps one of them has already died, but I also cannot find that one." That is the voice of despair of one who lived in surroundings in which the spirit has not been cultivated. Therefore, such souls remain in the dark in relation to the spiritual world and they cannot even be seen from the spiritual world.

On the other hand, when an initiate finds souls who have left others behind in the physical world, and who cultivated a spiritual life such as spiritual science, then he finds the dead can perceive the souls after death and communicate with them.

The so-called dead need the living, for otherwise they would only be able to behold themselves on earth, that is, their own life that has run its course. This explains the deed of love that we can perform for the dead by reading spiritually to them, not aloud, but in thoughts, by imagining the dead here with us in thought. In this way we can read to a number of dead at one and the same time, with or without a book, and thereby perform a considerable deed of love for them. The thoughts must be related to a spiritual content, otherwise they have no meaning for the dead. These thoughts create an external world for the dead that he can perceive. To think chemical laws and so forth has no sense because these laws are meaningless in the spiritual world.

It is also impossible, as one might easily imagine, to learn any more spiritual science after death because spiritual science after all contains spiritual ideas. We can do a great service to souls who have already heard something of spiritual science by reading cycles of lectures to them. Although such souls are able to perceive a spiritual world, they are nevertheless not able to form concepts and ideas that one can only acquire here on earth.

Let us take an example. There are beings known as bodhisattvas, lofty human beings who are far advanced and who incarnate repeatedly on the earth until they have ascended to the rank of buddhahood. As long as a bodhisattva dwells within a physical body, he lives as a man among men, as a spiritual benefactor of mankind. Even here on earth he has a special task, which is to teach not only the living but the dead and even the beings of the higher hierarchies. This is due to the fact that the content of earthly theosophy can only be acquired on earth within a physical body. It can then be made use of in the spiritual world but it must be attained within a physical body.

After their deaths, bodhisattvas can only in exceptional cases assist the progress of other beings, beings in the spiritual world who have already received the spark of the spirit here on earth. Theosophy cannot arise through the spiritual world as such. It only arises on earth and can then be taken upward by man into the spiritual world.

This can be understood if we consider that animals, for example, see everything on the earth as men do, but cannot understand what they see. Supersensible beings can only behold the supersensible world but cannot understand it. Concepts and ideas of the spiritual world can only arise on earth, and they ray forth like a light into the spiritual world. This enables one to understand rightly the meaning of the earth. The earth is neither a mere transitional stage, nor a vale of despair, but it exists so that on it a spiritual knowledge can be developed which can then be carried upward into the spiritual worlds.

Lightning Source UK Ltd.
Milton Keynes UK
UKOW05f0638080114

224160UK00001B/39/P